CW00952649

1 MONTH OF
FREE
READING

at

www.ForgottenBooks.com

By purchasing this book you are eligible for one month membership to ForgottenBooks.com, giving you unlimited access to our entire collection of over 1,000,000 titles via our web site and mobile apps.

To claim your free month visit:
www.forgottenbooks.com/free912340

* Offer is valid for 45 days from date of purchase. Terms and conditions apply.

ISBN 978-0-266-93607-7
PIBN 10912340

This book is a reproduction of an important historical work. Forgotten Books uses
state-of-the-art technology to digitally reconstruct the work, preserving the original format
whilst repairing imperfections present in the aged copy. In rare cases, an imperfection in
the original, such as a blemish or missing page, may be replicated in our edition. We do,
however, repair the vast majority of imperfections successfully; any imperfections that
remain are intentionally left to preserve the state of such historical works.

Forgotten Books is a registered trademark of FB &c Ltd.
Copyright © 2018 FB &c Ltd.
FB &c Ltd, Dalton House, 60 Windsor Avenue, London, SW19 2RR.
Company number 08720141. Registered in England and Wales.

For support please visit www.forgottenbooks.com

SALE NUMBER 4276

FREE PUBLIC EXHIBITION

From Saturday, November 14, to Time of Sale
Weekdays 9 to 6 • Sunday 2 to 5

PUBLIC SALE

Friday and Saturday
November 20 and 21
at 2 p. m. each day

EXHIBITION & SALE AT THE

AMERICAN ART ASSOCIATION
ANDERSON GALLERIES · INC
30 East 57th Street
New York City

Sales Conducted by
HIRAM H. PARKE • OTTO BERNET • H. E. RUSSELL, JR
1936

VIEW OF CHAPEL SHOWING SPANISH BAROQUE ALTAR

[NUMBER 424]

GOTHIC AND RENAISSANCE ART

*Including Notable Spanish Wood Carvings
and Other Sculptures
Sumptuous Textiles and Tapestries
Stained Glass ₁ Paintings*

IMPORTANT K'ANG-HSI PORCELAINS

*Notably Rare and Valuable Famille Noire Vases and
A Choice Peachbloom Amphora*

FRENCH, SPANISH, ITALIAN FURNITURE
A SPANISH BAROQUE ALTAR
AND CEILING

Property of

MRS HERBERT SHIPMAN

*Removed from Her Residences at
Newport, R. I., and The River House, New York*

SOLD BY HER ORDER

❧

Public Sale
November 20 and 21 at 2 p. m.

AMERICAN ART ASSOCIATION
ANDERSON GALLERIES · INC
1936

PRICED CATALOGUES

A priced copy of this catalogue may be
obtained for one dollar for each
session of the sale

PRINTED IN THE U. S. A.

CONDITIONS OF SALE

The property listed in this catalogue will be offered and sold subject to the following terms and conditions:

1. The word "Company", wherever used in these Conditions of Sale, means the American Art Association-Anderson Galleries, Inc.

2. The Company has exercised reasonable care to catalogue and describe correctly the property to be sold, but it does not warrant the correctness of description, genuineness, authenticity or condition of said property.

3. Unless otherwise announced by the auctioneer at the time of sale, all bids are to be for a single article even though more than one article is included under a numbered item in the catalogue. If, however, the articles under any one numbered item are designated as a "Lot" then bids are to be for the lot irrespective of the number of articles described in such item.

4. The highest bidder accepted by the auctioneer shall be the buyer. In the event of any dispute between bidders, the auctioneer may, in his discretion, determine who is the successful bidder, and his decision shall be final; or the auctioneer may reoffer and resell the article in dispute.

5. Any bid which is not commensurate with the value of the article offered, or which is merely a nominal or fractional advance over the previous bid, may be rejected by the auctioneer, in his discretion, if in his judgment such bid would be likely to affect the sale injuriously.

6. The name and address of the buyer of each article, or lot, shall be given to the Company immediately following the sale thereof, and payment of the whole purchase price, or such part thereof as the Company may require, shall be immediately made by the purchaser thereof. If the foregoing condition, or any other applicable condition herein, is not complied with, the sale may, at the option of the Company, be cancelled, and the article, or lot, reoffered for sale.

7. Unless the sale is advertised and announced as an unrestricted sale, or a sale without reserve, consignors reserve the right to bid.

8. Except as herein otherwise provided, title will pass to the highest bidder upon the fall of the auctioneer's hammer, and thereafter the property is at the purchaser's sole risk and responsibility.

9. Articles sold and not paid for in full and not taken by noon of the day following the sale may be turned over by the Company to a carrier to be delivered to a storehouse for the account and risk of the purchaser, and at his cost. If the purchase price has not been so paid in full, the Company may either cancel the sale, and any partial payment already made shall thereupon be forfeited as liquidated damages, or it may resell the same, without notice to the buyer and for his account and risk, and hold him responsible for any deficiency.

[A]

10. If for any cause whatsoever any article sold cannot be delivered, or cannot be delivered in as good condition as the same may have been at the time of sale, the sale will be cancelled, and any amount that may have been paid on account of the sale will be returned to the purchaser.

11. In addition to the purchase price, the buyer will be required to pay the New York City sales tax, unless the buyer is exempt from the payment thereof.

12. The Company, subject to these Conditions of Sale and to such terms and conditions as it may prescribe, but without charge for its services, will undertake to make bids for responsible parties approved by it. Requests for such bidding must be given with such clearness as to leave no room for misunderstanding as to the amount to be bid and must state the catalogue number of the item and the name or title of the article to be bid on. If bids are to be made on several articles listed as one item in the catalogue, the request should state the amount to be bid on each article, unless the item contains the notation "Lot", in which case the request should state the amount to be bid "For the Lot". The Company reserves the right to decline to undertake to make such bids.

13. The Company will facilitate the employment of carriers and packers by purchasers but will not be responsible for the acts of such carriers or packers in any respect whatsoever.

14. These Conditions of Sale cannot be altered except in writing by the Company or by public announcement by the auctioneer at the time of sale.

SALES CONDUCTED BY HIRAM H. PARKE, OTTO BERNET, AND H. E. RUSSELL JR.

AMERICAN ART ASSOCIATION
ANDERSON GALLERIES · INC
30 EAST 57TH STREET · NEW YORK

Telephone PLaza 3-1269   *Cable* Artgal *or* Andauction

HIRAM H. PARKE · *President*

Otto Bernet · *Vice-President*   Arthur Swann · *2nd Vice-President*

[A]

ORDER OF SALE

Page

FIRST SESSION

Friday, November 20, 1936, at 2 p. m.

PASSEMENTERIE, DAMASKS AND BROCATELLES
VELVETS AND EMBROIDERIES

1. FOUR ITALIAN GOLD-, SILK-, AND SILVER-EMBROIDERED ESCUTCHEONS
A pair crested with coronets and two with prelates' hats with pendent *fiocci.* [Lot.]

2. GOLD- AND SILK-EMBROIDERED ESCUTCHEON
Spanish, Late XVII Century
Arms of a prince of Spain, with coronet.

3. FIVE LENGTHS OF GOLD LACE   *French, XVIII Century*
Narrow laces of fine quality, with rococo shell and floral designs.
[Lot.]   *Total length, about 67 yards*

4. EIGHTEEN SILK TASSELS   *French and Italian, XVII-XVIII Century*
Set of five fine large baroque tassels in yellow silk; two pairs of yellow silk and silver tassels; nine small tassels in pastel colors. [Lot.]

5. TWO LENGTHS OF CRIMSON SILK AND GOLD FRINGE
Italian, XVIII Century
With twisted gold threads and crimson tassels; four pieces. [Lot.]
Total length, about 17 yards

6. LENGTH OF GOLD GALLOON   *Italian, XVIII Century*
With chevron design in a tan ground; twenty-one pieces. [Lot.]
Total length, about 49½ yards; width, 2 inches

7. LENGTH OF GOLD GALLOON   *Italian Baroque*
Patterned with latticed cartouches alternating with diamond motives; probably nineteenth century; four pieces. [Lot.]
Total length, about 44 yards; width, 2 inches

8. LENGTH OF GOLD GALLOON
Broad band galloon, with geometrical design enclosing lozenge motives; four pieces. [Lot.]
Total length, about 37 yards; width, 3½ inches

9. LENGTH OF GOLD GALLOON — *Italian, XVII Century*
Patterned with an undulating design of foliage enclosing small blossoms; six pieces. [Lot.]
Total length, about 18 yards; width, 3¼ inches

10. THREE LENGTHS OF SILVER LACE — *French, XVIII Century*
Fine lace, with rococo scallop-shell and trellis design; seven pieces. [Lot.] *Total length, about 19 yards*

11. LENGTH OF GOLD GALLOON
Band galloon, with geometrical trellis design.
Total length, about 54 yards; width, 2¼ inches

12. LENGTH OF GIMP
Braid with velvet design in colors, depicting recurrent cartouches of mermaids; four pieces. [Lot.]
Total length, about 15½ yards; width, 2¼ inches

13. LOT OF GOLD FRINGE
Assorted pieces; as exhibited. [Lot.]

14. SIX LENGTHS OF SILK GIMP AND FRINGE
Crimson, green, and golden yellow braid gimp; yellow silk ball fringe; yellow silk braid fringe; and gimp fringe in blue, rose, green, and yellow silk, of the eighteenth century. As exhibited. [Lot.]

15. LOT OF ANTIQUE GOLD GALLOONS
Narrow galloons, in about eight different patterns, as exhibited; twenty-three pieces. [Lot.] *Total length, about 53 yards*

16. PAIR GOLD EMBROIDERY ESCUTCHEONS *Italian, Early XVIII Century*
Coroneted escutcheon worked with a mortuary emblem and with pendant of twin serpents.

17. PAIR GOLD EMBROIDERY ESCUTCHEONS *Italian, Early XVIII Century*
Similar to the preceding.

18. PAIR GOLD EMBROIDERY ESCUTCHEONS *Italian, Early XVIII Century*
Escutcheons worked with mortuary emblems and surmounted by a coronet; in gold, heightened with colored silks.

19. PAIR APPLIQUÉ-EMBROIDERED CRIMSON SATIN
ECCLESIASTICAL COLLARS   *Spanish, Late XVI Century*
Crimson satin appliqué in yellow and white silk with Renaissance
volutes of lilies.

20. FRAPPÉ CRIMSON VELVET CUSHION   *Italian, XVII Century*
Stamped with a bold design of interlacing leaf scrollings.

21. RENAISSANCE GOLD-NEEDLEPAINTED ORPHREY *Italian, XVI* Century
Finely needlepainted in gold and shaded silks with figures of SS. Lucy
and Mary Magdalene, within niches, and the Savior bearing His cross.
Length, 50 inches; width, 10 inches

22. GOLD- AND SILVER-EMBROIDERED GREEN VELVET APPAREL
Italian Renaissance
Olive green velvet, embroidered with a circular cartouche of flowers
surrounded by foliage and a vine border.
Length, 23½ inches; width, 22 inches

23. THREE VELVET PANELS WITH ITALIAN EMBROIDERY ESCUTCHEONS
Appliqué escutcheons in gold and colored silks, on ruby and plum red
velvet. [Lot.]

24. GREEN AND CRIMSON SILK DAMASK ARMORIAL CUSHION
XVII-XVIII Century
Border of green silk damask enclosing a crimson damask panel with
appliqué-embroidered escutcheon of a Spanish prince.

25. CRIMSON VELVET ARMORIAL CUSHION   *Italian, XVII Century*
Appliqué with a gold papal escutcheon, embroidered with green Spanish
brocatelle.

26. FOUR GOLD-EMBROIDERED CHALICE COVERS
French and Italian, XVIII Century
Variously embroidered with a cross and glory, within floral and ro-
coco borders. [Lot.]

27. FIVE LENGTHS OF CRIMSON SATIN LAMPAS BORDER
Woven in black and fawn silks with scrolling branches terminating in
lotus blossoms.   *Length of each, 7 feet; width, 10 inches*

28. TWO PAIRS CRIMSON SILK BROCATELLE CUSHIONS

Italian, XVII Century

Patterned with large symmetrical designs of flowers and foliage and paneled with gold galloon.

29. PAIR CRIMSON SILK BROCATELLE CUSHIONS   *Italian, XVII Century*

Design very similar to the preceding.

30. TWO SMALL ARMORIAL PANELS

Panel of green velvet with appliqué Italian escutcheon; and crimson silk damask drum trapping, embroidered with the royal arms of England.

31. SIX LENGTHS OF CRIMSON AND OLD GOLD SILK BROCATELLE BORDER

Spanish, XVII Century

Crimson satin on an old gold ground, developing a design of spatulate frameworks, enclosing stars, and large five-petaled blossoms.

Total length, 51 feet 5 inches; width, 11 inches

32. FIVE CRIMSON VELVET ARMORIAL SEAT COVERS

Italian, XVIII Century

Four appliqué with gold-embroidered coroneted escutcheons. [Lot.]

33. PAIR GENOESE CRIMSON VELVET CUSHIONS
WITH SIXTEENTH CENTURY EMBROIDERY

Each appliqué with an ecclesiastical collar worked with Renaissance leaf scrollings.

34. TWELVE SMALL MOSS GREEN VELVET PANELS

Genoese, XVII Century

Velvet of good quality. [Lot.]   *11 inches square*

35. TWELVE SMALL MOSS GREEN VELVET PANELS

Genoese, XVII Century

Similar to the preceding. [Lot.]

36. TWELVE SMALL MOSS GREEN VELVET PANELS

Genoese, XVII Century

Similar to the preceding. [Lot.]

37. FOURTEEN SMALL MOSS GREEN VELVET PANELS
Genoese, XVII Century
Similar to the preceding. [Lot.]

38. LENGTH OF MOSS GREEN VELVET BORDER   *Genoese, XVII Century*
Velvet similar to the preceding; comprising nine pieces. [Lot.]
Total length, about 28 yards

39. TWO PAIRS GREEN SILK BROCATELLE CUSHIONS
Italian, XVII Century
Patterned with huge Louis XIV designs of flowers and foliage flanked
by cornucopiae.

40. PAIR EMPIRE GOLD APPLIQUÉ-EMBROIDERED SAPPHIRE BLUE
VELVET VALANCES   *Italian, circa* 1810
Light blue velvet, appliqué-embroidered in gold galloon with a fretted
border surmounted by a row of tulip palmettes within pointed arches.
Length, 12 *feet; depth,* 15 *inches*
From French & Co., Inc., New York

41. EMPIRE GOLD APPLIQUÉ-EMBROIDERED SAPPHIRE BLUE
VELVET VALANCE   *Italian, circa* 1810
Similar to the preceding.   *Length,* 15 *feet; depth,* 15 *inches*
From French & Co., Inc., New York

42. PAIR CRIMSON CUT AND UNCUT VELVET CUSHIONS   *Italian Baroque*
Patterned with a symmetrical spray of flowers and foliage and paneled
in gold galloon.

43. PAIR CRIMSON CUT AND UNCUT VELVET CUSHIONS   *Italian Baroque*
Design of the preceding.

44. PAIR CRIMSON CUT AND UNCUT VELVET CUSHIONS   *Italian Baroque*
Design of the preceding, but larger.

45. SCUTARI JARDINIERE VELVET PANEL   *XVII Century*
Woven with an oval floral medallion in green and salmon pink, within
a geometrical border.   *Length,* 46 *inches; width,* 26 *inches*

46. Green Velvet and Appliqué-embroidered
Embroidery Banner   *Spanish Baroque*
A circular medallion of gold floral embroidery enclosing a needle-
painted figure of a saint, appliqué upon a green velvet panel, with a
Renaissance appliqué-embroidered silk border and gold fringe.
Length, 56 inches; width, 36 inches

35 —

47. Green Silk Damask Runner   *Italian, Late XVII Century*
Myrtle green satin ground woven with a symmetrical design of pairs
of cornucopiae, blossoms, and leaves forming frameworks enclosing
palmettes.   *Length, 6 feet 7 inches; width, 25 inches*

30 –

48. Fine Apple Green Velvet and Gold- and Silk-needlepainted
Table Cover   *Italian, XVI-XVII Century*
Seventeenth century light green velvet, centred with a panel of seven
vignettes, framed by cornucopiae, enclosing needlepainted figures of
the Madonna and Child and male and female saints including SS.
Gregory, Lucy, and Lawrence. Broad gold galloon border.
Length, 7 feet 6 inches; width, 28 inches

160 –

49. Golden Yellow Silk Damask Coverlet
Spanish, Late XVIII Century
Patterned with a close allover diamond trellis design enclosing single
blossoms.   *Length, 6 feet 10 inches; width, 6 feet*

40 –

50. Ivory and Gold Brocade Runner   *Venetian Baroque*
Ivory satin ground woven with vertical ribs supporting elaborately
curled gold leafage and tiny blossoms woven in pastel silks.
Length, 9 feet; width, 20 inches

110

51. Eight Pieces of Genoese Moss Green Velvet
Italian, XVII Century
Lustrous green velvet, in shaped pieces; as exhibited. [Lot.]

35 —

6

Spanish Baroque
closing a needle-
vet panel, with a
d fringe.
width, 36 inches

XVII Century
design of pairs
works enclosing
width, 25 inches

-NEEDLEPAINTED
VII-XVII Century
a panel of seven
painted figures of
including SS.
der.
width, 28 inches

XVIII Century
enclosing single
width, 6 feet

Venetian Baroque
elaborately
S.
width, 20 inches

on, XVII Century
[Lot.]

52. PLUM VELVET AND SIXTEENTH CENTURY SILK NEEDLEPOINT PANEL
Plum velvet centred with a narrow panel worked in *gros point* with a
Renaissance floral design, the ground unfinished; gold galloon.
Length, 59 inches; width, 29 inches

53. GOLD-NEEDLEPAINTED HOOD AND DRAP D'OR
APPLIQUÉ-EMBROIDERED ORPHREY   *Spanish, XVI-XVII Century*
Hood needlepainted in gold and shaded silks with a circular medallion
of the Annunciation, surrounded by salamanders, birds, and foliage;
orphrey of *drap d'or* appliqué-embroidered in crimson velvet with serpentine scrolls of interlacing leafage.   *Length, 14 feet*

54. MOSS GREEN VELVET CAPE   *French, XVIII Century*
Cut in the pattern of a cape and unfinished.

55. IVORY SILK AND GOLD BROCADE CHASUBLE
Venetian, Early XVIII Century
Ivory damask ground brocaded in gold and colored silks with serpen-
tines formed of large leaves, blossoms, and pagodas; paneled with gold
galloon.

56. GREEN VELVET FRONTAL   *French, XVIII Century*
Apple green velvet, paneled and bordered with gold galloon; gold
fringe; lined and backed.   *Length, 7 feet 4 inches; depth, 28 inches*

57. GREEN VELVET FRONTAL   *French, XVIII Century*
Similar to the preceding.

58. PAIR SAGE GREEN AND IVORY BROCATELLE COVERS
Italian, XVII Century
Ivory ground woven in green with palmettes and pairs of cornucopiae;
gold galloon and fringe.   *Length, 56 inches; width, 22 inches*

59. GOLD APPLIQUÉ-EMBROIDERED CRIMSON VELVET RUNNER
Portuguese, XVII Century
Crimson velvet appliqué-embroidered with *drap d'or* to a design of
large skeleton palmettes, pairs of pomegranates, and sprays of *ajouré*
leaves; gold fringe at ends.   *Length, 9 feet; width, 20½ inches*

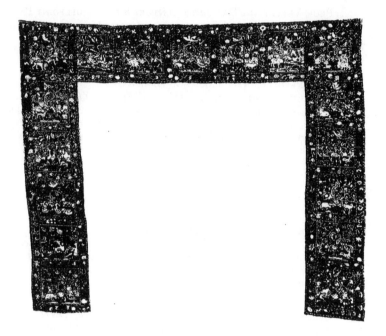

[NUMBER 60]

60. ELIZABETHAN PETIT POINT AND GROS POINT CANTONNIÈRE
Beautifully worked in deep colors with seventeen square vignettes of
wild animals and birds within landscapes; framed by tawny red floral
borders.   *External height, 5 feet 9 inches; length, 7 feet 2 inches*
From Lenygon & Morant, Inc., New York

[See illustration]

61. MYRTLE GREEN SILK DAMASK COVERLET   *Italian, XVIII Century*
Woven with sprays of latticed leaves, small flowers, and sprouting
pods, upon a satin ground; four widths.
    Length, 7 feet 10 inches; width, 6 feet 10 inches

8

62. THREE LENGTHS OF ANTIQUE CRIMSON VELVET
Good patina; some stains and wears. [Lot.]
Total length, about 11½ yards; width, 28 inches

63. SIX GREEN AND IVORY SILK BROCATELLE COVERS
Italian, XVII Century
Ivory ground, woven in sage green with large Louis XIV designs of spatulate and latticed palmettes; gold galloon.
Length, about 47 inches; width, 22 inches

64. ELEVEN GREEN AND IVORY SILK BROCATELLE COVERS
Italian, XVII Century
Designs very similar to the preceding; gold galloon.
Lengths, from 19 to 25 inches; width, 22 inches

65. LYONS CRIMSON VELVET VALANCE
Long valance trimmed with gold galloon and fringe; together with a small valance of sixteenth century Genoese crimson velvet.
Length, 15 feet 4 inches; depth, 14 inches

66. PAIR CRIMSON VELVET AND BROCATELLE COVERS
Spanish, XVII Century
Crimson velvet centring a narrow panel of brocatelle woven in crimson satin on a golden yellow ground with spatulate frameworks enclosing stars.
Length, 53 inches; width, 28 inches

67. CRIMSON VELVET TABLE COVER   *Genoese, XVII Century*
Bordered with wide gold galloon.   *Length, 6 feet; width, 24 inches*

68. CRIMSON VELVET TABLE COVER   *Genoese, XVII Century*
Similar to the preceding.

9

[NUMBER 69]

69. CRIMSON AND GOLD APPLIQUÉ-EMBROIDERED ARMORIAL FRONTAL
Spanish, Late XVI Century
Crimson silk panel embroidered with gold cordonnets and silver bullion
in a lattice of ogivals enclosing floral vases and centred with an escutcheon with prelate's hat and *fiocci;* bordered at top and sides with crimson velvet, appliqué-embroidered in gold with Renaissance lilies and
two matching escutcheons and centring a needlepainted medallion of
S. John the Baptist. *Length, 7 feet 6 inches; depth, 42 inches*

2 50 -

[See illustration]

70. LENGTH OF CRIMSON SILK BROCATELLE *Italian, Late XVII Century*
In two pieces. Woven with a satin design of large peony blossoms and
pairs of pomegranates supported by vases and baskets.
Lengths, 18 feet 7 inches and 5 feet 3 inches; width, 25 inches

17 50

71. ROSE CRIMSON VELVET VALANCE *Genoese, XVII Century*
Plain scalloped valance of five points.
Length, 6 feet 10 inches; depth, 20 inches

20 -

10

72. GOLD APPLIQUÉ-EMBROIDERED AND NEEDLEPAINTED GARNET
VELVET ANTEPENDIUM   *Italian Renaissance Style*
Paneled and appliqué-embroidered in gold and silver with sprays of
lilies centred by a palmette, the side panels with figures of a lady and
a gentleman in fifteenth century costumes, standing in landscapes.
Border embroidered with Renaissance strapwork and lilies and portrait
vignettes.   *Length, 8 feet 4 inches; depth, 38 inches*

/00-

73. GREEN SILK DAMASK AND APPLIQUÉ-EMBROIDERED
VELVET COVERLET   *Italian, circa 1700*
Light green damask with a satin ground woven with repeated scrolling
branches of flowers and latticed leaves; border of olive green velvet
appliqué-embroidered in silver bullion with a vine of lilies springing
from shells at the corners.
Length, 7 feet 3 inches; width, 5 feet 6 inches

50-

74. PAIR CRIMSON VELVET AND GOLD NEEDLEPAINTED RUNNERS
Italian, XVII Century
Crimson velvet, centring two orphrey panels of later date in the Italian
Renaissance style, worked in gold and colored silks with circular medal-
lions depicting the Flagellation, the Scourging of Christ, Christ and
S. Veronica, the Crucifixion, the Deposition, and the Resurrection.
Length, 7 feet 9 inches; width, 15 inches

2/0-

75. LOUIS PHILIPPE CRIMSON SILK DAMASK COVERLET
French, circa 1840
Satin ground woven with cartouches supporting roses and enclosing
naturalistic nosegays; four widths; silk fringe.
Length, 10 feet 3 inches; width, 7 feet 2 inches

3/⁄0/

76. NEEDLEPAINTED AND APPLIQUÉ-EMBROIDERED CRIMSON
VELVET ANTEPENDIUM   *Italian, XVI Century*
Crimson velvet appliqué-embroidered with panels of lilies and scrolled
frames enclosing saints, the two central figures of S. Agatha and S.
Catherine; side panels with smaller roundels of later date, depicting
saints. Gold fringe.   *Length, 58 inches; depth, 44 inches*

2/0-

11

[NUMBER 77]

77. CRIMSON AND OLD GOLD CUT VELVET HANGING

Italian, XVII Century

Stitched old gold ground, bearing a design in *ciselé* crimson velvet of large waving leaves and peonies; three widths.

Length, 9 feet 6 inches; width, 5 feet

[See illustration]

12

78. PAIR CRIMSON AND OLD GOLD CUT VELVET COLUMN HANGINGS
Italian, XVII Century
Design of the preceding; gold fringe. *Length, 8 feet; width, 20 inches*

79. PAIR CRIMSON AND OLD GOLD CUT VELVET COLUMN HANGINGS
Italian, XVII Century
Similar to the preceding.

80. CRIMSON AND OLD GOLD CUT VELVET COVER   *Italian, XVII Century*
Design of the preceding.   *Length, 8 feet 4 inches; width, 20 inches*

81. CHARTREUSE GREEN VELVET PANEL   *French, XVIII Century*
Paneled and bordered with wide gold galloon.
Length, 6 feet 8½ inches; width, 45 inches

82. CHARTREUSE GREEN VELVET PANEL   *French, XVIII Century*
Very similar to the preceding.

83. CHARTREUSE GREEN VELVET PANEL   *French, XVIII Century*
Similar to the preceding.

84. TWO LENGTHS OF CRIMSON SILK DAMASK
Italian, Late XVII Century
Satin ground, woven with a huge symmetrical design of a flowering palmette enclosed within foliage springing from long stems supported by pairs of diapered pomegranates and leaves.
Lengths, 21 feet 4 inches and 7 feet 8 inches; width, 33 inches

85. CRIMSON VELVET AND NEEDLEPAINTED BANNER
Spanish, XVII Century
Dark crimson velvet scalloped banner, appliqué with a needlepainted representation of the Holy Trinity, worked in gold, silver, and silks.
Length, 56 inches; width, 37 inches

86. TWO LENGTHS OF ROSE SILK DAMASK   *Italian, Late XVI Century*
Satin ground, woven with a formal pattern of coroneted ogivals enclosing pomegranates; faded and with repairs.
Total length, 16 feet 6 inches; width, 21½ inches

87. CRIMSON AND IVORY SILK LAMPAS COVER
Crimson satin ground brocaded in pale gray with curving stems of Chinese peonies; two widths. *Length, 6 feet 5 inches; width, 57 inches*

13

88. LENGTH OF RUBY VELVET   *Italian, XVIII Century*
    Patinated velvet, with small tear.   *Length, 11 feet; width, 20 inches*

89. TWO LEAF GREEN SILK DAMASK COVERLETS
                                    French or Italian, XVIII Century
    Satin ground, woven with a delicate symmetrical design of latticed
    vases, supporting a profuse array of pinks and wild roses; slightly
    faded. In four widths.
    Lengths, 5 feet 10 inches and 7 feet 8 inches; width, 6 feet 10 inches

90. TWO LEAF GREEN SILK DAMASK COVERLETS
                                    French or Italian, XVIII Century
    Design of the preceding; slightly faded; in three and four widths.
                        Length, 5 feet 8 inches; width, 5 feet 1 inch
                        Length, 6 feet 6 inches; width, 6 feet 10 inches

91. LEAF GREEN SILK DAMASK COVERLET
                                    French or Italian, XVIII Century
    Design of the preceding; slightly faded; five widths.
                        Length, 10 feet 6 inches; width, 5 feet 8 inches

92. TWO LENGTHS OF ROSE VELVET   *French, XVIII Century*
    One piece edged with gold galloon.
                    Lengths, 8 feet 8 inches and 8 feet 10 inches; width, 35 inches

93. MOSS GREEN AND JARDINIERE VELVET HANGING
                                    Italian, XVII-XVIII Century
    Lustrous green velvet (repaired), bordered with a side panel of jar-
    diniere velvet developing rose and yellow blossoms and green leafage
    upon an ivory ground. Gold galloon. Lined and interlined.
                        Length, 9 feet 4 inches; width, 47 inches

94. GREEN VELVET ANTEPENDIUM   *French, XVIII Century*
    Light green velvet, bordered with gold galloon and fringed.
                        Length, 5 feet 10 inches; depth, 29 inches

95. CRIMSON SILK DAMASK COVERLET   *Italian, XVII-XVIII Century*
    Satin ground, woven with a Louis XIV design of large blossoms en-
    closed within huge ogivals of curling leaves; gold galloon.
                        Length, 10 feet 8 inches; width, 48 inches

14

96. PAIR LYONS CRIMSON VELVET HANGINGS
Heavy velvet, bordered with wide gold galloon; lined.
Length, 8 feet; width, 26½ inches

97. LEAF GREEN SILK DAMASK COVERLET   *Italian, Late XVII Century*
Light green damask with satin ground and Louis XIV design, exhibiting large floral palmettes enclosed within frameworks and supported upon twin C-scrolls. Four widths.
Length, 9 feet; width, 8 feet 4 inches

98. EMPIRE SILVER-EMBROIDERED SAPPHIRE BLUE VELVET HANGING
Italian, circa 1810
Lustrous blue velvet appliqué with silver bullion embroidery, developing curling and radiating branches of blossoms springing from a central leaf palmette and supporting a palm tree and plaquette inscribed *Quasi Palma*. Base border of vases and Empire motives and fringed.
Height, 7 feet 5 inches; width, 58 inches

99. CRIMSON SILK DAMASK HANGING   *Italian Baroque*
Satin ground, woven with a naturalistic design of large palmettes enclosed within frameworks of curling leafage. Bordered with silk galloon, and rounded at the base. Four widths.
Length, 8 feet 6 inches; width, 9 feet 6 inches

100. GOLD APPLIQUÉ-EMBROIDERED CRIMSON VELVET COVERLET
WITH THE ROYAL SPANISH COAT OF ARMS
Spanish, XVII-XVIII Century
Crimson velvet appliqué with a large coroneted escutcheon, flanked with cornucopiae, and with bullion embroidery of large vases of flowers at the corners. Lace galloon.
Length, 9 feet 7 inches; width, 6 feet 6 inches

101. FOUR LENGTHS GOLD APPLIQUÉ-EMBROIDERED RUBY
VELVET VALANCE   *Spanish, XVI-XVII Century*
Appliqué-embroidered with gold galloon, in two designs: one with a vine of fan motives, the other with a vine of trefoils. [Lot.]
Total length of three, 20 feet 6 inches; depth, 12 inches
Length of one, 13 feet 8 inches; depth, 15 inches

15

102. PAIR GOLD APPLIQUÉ-EMBROIDERED CRIMSON
CUT VELVET VALANCES   *Portuguese, XVII Century*
Crimson cut velvet ground exhibiting Louis XIV floral designs,
appliqué-embroidered in *drap d'or* with large symmetrical floral plants,
in three scalloped panels.   *Length, 6 feet 9 inches; depth, 30 inches*

3 5

103. PAIR CRIMSON SILK DAMASK AND BROCATELLE HANGINGS
Italian, Late XVII Century
Crimson damask with satin ground bearing a Louis XIV design of
huge frameworks formed of curling leafage and pomegranates; Spanish brocatelle border on one side, with a design of spatulate palmettes
enclosing stars woven in crimson and old gold. Gold galloon.
Length, 9 feet 6 inches; width, 55 inches

3 5

104. CHINESE GOLD- AND SILK-EMBROIDERED CRIMSON SATIN
TEMPLE HANGING OF IMPORTANT SIZE   *Circa 1830*
Woven in gold thread and shaded silks with figures of the Eighteen
Lohan and other personages, surrounding a panel of lengthy inscrip-
tions in golden yellow silk; the whole within a border of lotus and
peony blossoms, fruits, and butterflies, the valance with a golden
dragon flanked by *fêng huang* birds.
Height, 14 feet 3 inches; width, 9 feet

3 o

105. GOLD- AND SILVER-EMBROIDERED SATIN COVERLET
Turkish, XIX Century
Rose satin, worked with a border of pinnacles and appliqué cartouches
of Turkish inscriptions, the field centring a pendented celadon floral
medallion with insignia.   *Length, 9 feet 6 inches; width, 6 feet*

3 5

106. PAIR GREEN SATIN AND VELVET HANGINGS
Chartreuse green satin, with a wide border of seventeenth century moss
green velvet, with gold galloon and fringe; lined and interlined.
Length, 10 feet; width, 39 inches

2 o

107. PAIR JARDINIERE VELVET COVERLETS   *Italian Baroque*
Ivory satin ground woven in pale pastel green, mauve, and orange with
large sprays of flowers and foliage, enclosed by curling leafage.
Length, 7 feet 6 inches; width, 49 inches

5 5

16

e, XVII Century
XIV floral designs,
...trical floral plants,
... depth, 30 inches

HANGINGS
Late XVII Century
... XIV design of
...granates; Span-
...ulate palmettes
... galoon.
... width, 55 inches

...SILKS
Circa 1830
... of the Eighteen
... lengthy inscrip-
... ler of lotus and
... with a golden
... ches; width, 9 feet

... k, XIX Century
... uphé cartouches
... celadon floral
... width, 6 feet

... oth century moss
... intertwined.
... width, 39 inches

Italian Baroque
... and orange with
... valance.
... width, 49 inches

108. QUILTED CHINTZ COVERLET   Circa 1840
Patterned with sprays of brown, sky blue, and tan blossoms, in an
aubergine ground.   *Length, 7 feet 6 inches; width, 5 feet 10 inches*

109. LOT OF GREEN CUT AND UNCUT VELVET *Italian XVII Century Style*
Woven with a bold Louis XIV design of cusped frameworks enclosing
floral palmettes and entwined with blossoms; four pieces of varying
sizes, as exhibited. [Lot.]

110. LOT OF ROSE CRIMSON VELVET   *Italian, XVII Century*
Six pieces of assorted sizes, as exhibited.
                        Total length, about 10½ yards; width, 20 inches

111. LOT OF CRIMSON AND WINE RED VELVET   *XVII-XVIII Century*
Seventeen pieces of varying sizes, as exhibited. [Lot.]

112. LOT OF ROSE CRIMSON SILK BROCATELLE   *Italian, XVII Century*
With bold Louis XIV design of peonies and foliage; twenty pieces of
varying size, as exhibited. [Lot.]

113. THREE DECORATIVE TEXTILES   *XVII Century*
Genoese velvet cover inset with rose lampas of later date; crimson
silk damask runner; and Portuguese valance embroidered with gold
palmettes and festoons on worn crimson velvet. [Lot.]

114. PLUSH CARRIAGE ROBE
Double-sided; one side in orange, the other in taupe plush.
                        Length, 5 feet 6 inches; width, 46 inches

115. NOVA SCOTIA RAISED HOOKED RUG
Worked with floral garland and horseshoe, captioned *Good Luck*, in
a tan floral cartouche.   *Length, 5 feet; width, 2 feet 7 inches*

17

GILDED AND POLYCHROMED STATUETTES
COLUMNS AND OTHER CARVINGS OF THE
XV TO XVIII CENTURIES

116. FOUR CARVED, GILDED, AND POLYCHROMED CORBEL FIGURES
Italian or Spanish, XVI Century
Kneeling figure of a cherub with gilded wings supporting a bracket.
Together with one plaster replica of the above. [Lot.]
Height, 11 inches

17 50

117. GOTHIC CARVED OAK SHRINE   *Flemish, Late XV Century*
Seated robed and hooded figure of the Virgin holding the Child,
within a canopy drawn back by two angels.
Height, 13½ inches; width, 9¾ inches

20 -

118. CARVED AND GILDED TRIPTYCH   *Spanish, XVI Century*
Portable folding shrine with quaint figures of a saintly pope flanked
by two other saints within niches.
Height, 11½ inches; length open, 18 inches

17 56

119. TWO GOTHIC SMALL CARVED, GILDED, AND POLYCHROMED GROUPS
South German, XV Century
One depicting Christ falling under the weight of the Cross, surrounded
by six mocking figures of quaintly robed townsfolk; the other the
mourning Virgin assisted and surrounded by groups of pious men and
women.   *Heights, 7 and 8¼ inches*
[See illustration]

75

120. CARVED, GILDED, AND POLYCHROMED STATUETTE OF A MONK
Spanish, XVII Century
Standing figure in sumptuously brocaded black and gold robes inscribed
CHARITAS, the face re-colored; square carved and gilded base.
Total height, 20 inches
[See illustration]

5 0

[120]   [121]   [122]

TOP ROW: NUMBER 119

121. Late Gothic Carved, Gilded, and Polychromed Group

Spanish, Early XVI Century

Robed and hooded figure of S. Anne in gilded nun's robes, holding a missal and, upon her right arm, the figures of the Virgin and Child.

Height, 14¼ *inches*

[See illustration]

122. Carved, Gilded, and Polychromed Statuette of a Bishop

Spanish, XVI Century

Standing robed and mounted figure holding a pastoral staff and giving a benediction with the right hand; carved and gilded plinth.

Height of statuette, 22 *inches*

[See illustration]

19

123. CARVED, GILDED, AND POLYCHROMED GROUP OF THE
VIRGIN AND CHILD   *Spanish, Late XVI Century*
Robed figure with voluminous green cloak and long flowing hair, hold-
ing the nude Child, Who caresses her cheek.   *Height, 14 inches*

2 5

124. THREE CARVED AND GILDED BAS RELIEFS
          Spanish, Late XVI Century
Each depicting the figure of a saint beneath a shell canopy. [Lot.]
       Heights, 20½ and 30 inches

3 5

125. EIGHT SMALL GILDED AND POLYCHROMED CARVINGS
          Spanish, mainly XVI Century
Small panels and fragments with figures of saints and acolytes, and
others as exhibited. [Lot.]

45

126. CARVED, GILDED, AND POLYCHROMED FIGURE OF GOD THE FATHER
          Spanish, XVII Century
Half-length figure, with outstretched arms, in gold-brocaded red robe
and green cloak, sheathed in a group of cherub heads.
       Height, 16 inches

/ 0

127. CARVED AND GILDED RELIQUARY CASKET
          Spanish, Late XVII Century
Oblong with open sides and scrolled and bracketed corners with carved
cherub heads; the cartouched dome surmounted by a bust.
       Height, 28 inches; width, 25½ inches

/ 0

128. PAIR CARVED, GILDED, AND POLYCHROMED STATUETTES
          Spanish(?), XVII Century
Bearded and mustached male figure wearing a curious hooded cloak
with loose sleeves and long lappeted skirt.   *Height, 20 inches*

/ 0

129. TWO CARVED AND GILDED WALL CARTOUCHES
          XVII-XVIII Century
One with painted escutcheon surrounded by gilded acanthus scrollings;
the other a *haut relief* medallion of S. Roch, with rococo cresting.
       Heights, 14¾ and 20 inches

2 0

130. CARVED, GILDED, AND POLYCHROMED STATUETTE
Spanish, XVII Century

Seated figure of a saintly monarch, probably S. Louis, in golden robe, painted with pink blossoms, and ermine cape; expounding from an open missal.   *Height, 18 inches*

131. CARVED, GILDED, AND POLYCHROMED STATUETTE OF THE
VIRGIN OF THE ASSUMPTION   *Spanish, XVIII Century*

Robed figure with clasped hands and long flowing hair, standing upon a crescent moon with cherub heads; gilded base.   *Total height, 26 inches*

132. CARVED, GILDED, AND POLYCHROMED STATUETTE
Spanish, XVII Century

Female saint in blue and gold cloak, with hood and gold damask gown; rich patina.   *Height, 24 inches*

133. CARVED, GILDED, AND POLYCHROMED HAUT RELIEF
Spanish, XVI Century

In three panels, depicting the Nativity, the Annunciation, and Christ appareled by the Virgin and S. John; between fluted Corinthian columns.   *Height, 13½ inches; length, 35 inches*

134. TWO PANELS FROM A GOTHIC CARVED LIMEWOOD ALTARPIECE
Spanish, XV Century

Depicting the mocking of Christ with surrounding crowds of hostile soldiery and citizens; framed.   *Total height, 25½ inches; length, 39½ inches*

135. CARVED, GILDED, AND POLYCHROMED STATUETTE OF THE SAVIOR
Spanish, XVIII Century

Wearing rich blue and gold robes, with rococo floral pattern, and golden cloak painted with flowers; standing upon a mass of clouds.   *Height, 33 inches*

136. THREE CARVED, GILDED, AND POLYCHROMED PANELS
Spanish, XVI Century

Haut relief depicting a Scriptural scene; and two small panels carved with cherubs, masks, and other Renaissance ornament. [Lot.]   *Heights, 17 and 23½ inches*

21

137. CARVED, GILDED, AND POLYCHROMED STATUETTE OF THE VIRGIN

Spanish, Late XVII Century

Standing figure with clasped hands, in flowing robes and swirling gold-brocaded cloak. *Height, 20 inches*

138. CARVED AND EBONIZED GROUP OF THE HOLY FAMILY

Spanish Baroque

Figures of S. Joseph and the Virgin with the Christ Child standing between them and the Holy Ghost above; on cartouched bracket support. *Height, 41 inches; width, 21 inches*

139. CARVED AND GILDED ESCUTCHEON *Italian, XVII Century*

Shield surmounted by a mural crown and garlanded with oak and bay leaves. *Height, 35 ½ inches; width, 33 inches*

140. CARVED, GILDED, AND POLYCHROMED GROUP, IN SHRINE

Spanish, circa 1600

Hooded figure, in richly brocaded golden robes, of S. Anne, carrying the Virgin and Child upon her left arm and a bowl of fruit in her right hand. In shrine richly carved with acanthus leafage, clusters of blossoms, and cherubs, and with canopy in the form of a crown. *Total height, 41 inches; width, 26 inches*

141. CARVED, GILDED, AND POLYCHROMED BAS RELIEF

Spanish or Italian, Late XVI Century

Depicting the Ascension, with the Savior appearing in the clouds above the heads of the affrighted Roman soldiers. *Height, 38 inches; width, 20¾ inches*

142. CARVED, GILDED, AND POLYCHROMED CRUCIFIX

Spanish, XVI Century

Cross carved with floral ornament, crocketed and terminating in four medallions of cherub heads; supporting a realistic figure of the Christ. Has stand. *Total height, 30 inches*

143. PAIR CARVED, GILDED, AND POLYCHROMED ALTAR STATUETTES

Italian, XVII Century

Walking figure in rich gilded robes, holding a cornucopia curving around the shoulder and designed for pricket. *Heights, 30 and 31 inches*

22

144. PAIR CARVED, GILDED, AND POLYCHROMED STATUETTES
Spanish, XVIII Century
Standing figure with long curling hair, wearing green robes caught up
at the knees; on acanthus-carved and gilded plinth.   *Height, 34 inches*

144A. PAIR CARVED AND GILDED COLUMNS   *Spanish, Late XVI Century*
Spirally fluted Corinthian column, the lower portion carved with
cherub heads and leaf scrollings.   *Height, 45 inches*

145. CARVED, GILDED, AND POLYCHROMED STATUETTE OF THE VIRGIN
Spanish, Late XVII Century
Standing richly robed figure clasping her hands, with crimson-lined
green and gold cloak caught up over her left arm; on base and stand
with carved cherub heads.   *Total height, 35 inches*

146. PAIR CARVED, GILDED, AND POLYCHROMED CANDELABRA FIGURES
Italian, XVII Century
Figures loosely draped in golden cloaks, each holding up a gilded
cornucopia; fitted for electricity; on plinth with carved and gilded leaf
volutes.   *Total height, 5 feet 2 inches*

147. PAIR CARVED, GILDED, AND POLYCHROMED COLUMNS
Spanish, XVII Century
Spirally fluted gilded column with Corinthian capital, the lower por-
tion with a carved and polychromed cherub head and scrolling leafage.
Height, 58 inches

148. CARVED, GILDED, AND POLYCHROMED STATUETTE
Spanish, Early XVII Century
Figure of a noble youth in green and gold corselet and red and gold
cloak, his right hand upraised; on carved and gilded plinth.
Height, 44 inches

149. PAIR BAROQUE CARVED AND GILDED COLUMNS
Spanish, Early XVII Century
Spirally twisted shaft entwined with vines and supporting a Corinthian
capital.   *Heights, 44 inches*

23

[NUMBER 150]

150. CARVED, GILDED, AND POLYCHROMED STATUE
OF THE VIRGIN AND CHILD   *Spanish(?), XVI Century*
Standing figure of the Virgin in richly draped golden cloak, holding
the nude Child upon her left arm; square gilded plinth.

Total height, 5 feet

[See illustration]

Note: This statue has achieved a wide reputation as a 'miracle-working'
image, due possibly to the curious illusion it offers, in certain lights, of opening
and shutting the eyes.

24

151. PAIR BAROQUE CARVED AND GILDED COLUMNS, FITTED AS LAMPS
Spanish, Early XVII Century
Spiraled column entwined with vines and supporting a Corinthian
capital; mounted on modern acanthus-carved base, and fitted for elec-
tricity. Together with an unmounted column to match. [Lot.]
Height, 52½ inches

152. PAIR CARVED, GILDED, AND POLYCHROMED ALTAR FIGURES
ON PLINTHS   *Spanish or Italian, Early XVII Century*
Kneeling figure in golden robes exposing one bare leg, the head tilted
upwards in adoration; on carved and gilded cartouche-shapd plinth
of baroque form.   *Total height, 56 inches*

153. PAIR BAROQUE CARVED AND GILDED COLUMNS   *Spanish, circa 1600*
Spirally twisted Corinthian columns, richly carved with vine leaves
and grapes.   *Height, 6 feet 2 inches*

154. FOUR CARVED CHESTNUT COLUMNS   *Spanish Baroque*
Spirally twisted composite column entwined with finely carved vines, in
which are bird figures. Together with a pair of corbels carved with a
figure sheathed in foliage and fruit. [Lot.]
Heights, 6 feet 4 inches and 6 feet 8 inches

155. SIX CARVED, GILDED, AND POLYCHROMED COLUMNS
Spanish, XVI-XVII Century
Spirally fluted columns, varying somewhat in design, the lower parts
with carved and polychromed leaf scrollings and cherub heads; one
fitted with a small glass *reliquaire*. [Lot.]
Heights, 45 inches to 6 feet 2 inches

156. SIX DECORATIVE CARVED WOOD PANELS
Two carved with English escutcheons amid leaf scrollings; three with a
cartouche surrounded by baroque foliage; and the sixth with a
'Romayne' medallion supporting *affrontés putti*. [Lot.]
Heights, 25½ to 31 inches

157. COLLECTION OF RENAISSANCE CARVED WOOD FRAGMENTS
Spanish, mainly XVI Century
Borders, panels, pilasters, etc., carved with scrolling leafage, mas-
carons, and the like, gilded and polychromed; as exhibited. [Lot.]

25

DECORATIVE OBJECTS
FRENCH, SPANISH, AND ITALIAN FURNITURE

158. JAPANESE CARVED IVORY TOILET BOX
Section of tusk finely carved and undercut upon the exterior with butterflies, insects, frogs, snails, and marine life, the cover with frog finial. *Height, 4¼ inches*

159. JAPANESE CARVED IVORY GROUP
A confused combat with figure of a woman grasping two swords, bending to attack a crouching robber, his accomplice wriggling upon the ground. *Height, 5 inches*

160. JAPANESE CARVED IVORY GROUP
Figure of an old crone leaning on a staff, accompanied by a nude male companion wrestling with a demon; signed. *Height, 6¼ inches*

161. CHINESE GILDED BRONZE BUDDHISTIC STATUETTE   *Ch'ien-lung*
Seated figure of a crowned Bodhisattva holding a vase of healing; re-coated with gold lacquer. *Height, 11¼ inches*

162. IVORY TANKARD, MOUNTED IN SILVER
Section of tusk with two loop handles, lightly engraved with a landscape with figure; mounted in chased silver with glass base. *Height, 5½ inches*

163. BOKHARA FAÏENCE CONIFORM BOWL   *XVII Century*
Painted in the interior with radial chrysanthemum petals in blue and green, the exterior glazed turquoise, with spiral hatchings; repaired. *Diameter, 12½ inches*

164. TWO WHITE FAÏENCE ARMORIAL PLAQUES   *Italian, XVIII Century*
Fluted plate painted with an escutcheon in majolica colors; repaired. *Diameters, 16 and 17¼ inches*

165. FOUR DELFT PLAQUES   *XVIII-XIX Century*
Three in blue and white, painted with garden vignettes and floral decoration; and one in polychrome in the Chinese taste, repaired. *Diameters, about 13½ inches*

26

NITURE

the exterior with
cover with frog
Height, 4¾ inches

ping two swords,
e wriggling upon
Height, 5 inches

d by a nude male
Height, 6½ inches

Ch'ien-lung
vase of healing;
ight, 11¼ inches

ized with a land-
base.
Height, 5½ inches

XVII Century
tals in blue and
gs; repaired.
ter, 12½ inches

XVIII Century
rs; repaired.
and 17¼ inches

III-XIX Century
and floral deco-
paired.
at 13½ inches

166. Two Repoussé Brass Plaques   *Flemish, XVI Century*
With bossed and spirally gadrooned *cavetti* surrounded by a chased
border of Gothic lettering.   *Diameters, 19¼ and 21 inches*

167. Pair Small Carved and Gilded Wall Mirrors
Spanish, XVII Century
Framed in curling baroque acanthus leaves.
Height, 13½ inches; width, 10 inches

168. Ispahan Blue and White Pottery Jar
Painted in cobalt blue with four medallion vignettes of flowers and
birds in the Chinese taste; base pierced.   *Height, 12½ inches*

169. Pair Small Carved and Gilded Wall Mirrors
Spanish, XVII Century
Upright mirror with acanthus and ribbon-carved frame.
Height, 16 inches; width, 14 inches

170. Landscape Sketch in Oils
Ralph Albert Blakelock, N.A., American: 1847-1919
Impression of sunset behind a dark line of trees.
Panel: Height, 5¼ inches; length, 9½ inches

171. Carved and Gilded Mirror Frame and Monstrance
Spanish Baroque
Carved with baroque scrolls of leafage. [Lot.]
Heights, 32 and 16½ inches

172. Pair Small Carved and Gilded Wall Mirrors   *Spanish Baroque*
Cartouche-shaped, bordered with leaf scrollings and carved floral ornament.   *Height, 18½ inches; width, 15 inches*

173. Pair Carved and Gilded Sanctuary Lamps
Italian or Spanish, Late XVII Century
Shaped and lobed, carved with blossoms and three cherub heads, to
which are attached the supporting chains.   *Height, about 37 inches*

174. Pair Carved and Gilded Altar Candlesticks
Italian, Late XVI Century
Gadrooned balustered and knopped standard, on acanthus-scrolled
trilateral base with paw feet; fitted for electricity.   *Height, 37 inches*

KINDLY READ CONDITIONS OF SALE IN FOREPART OF CATALOGUE

175. CARVED AND GILDED WALL MIRROR   *Spanish, XVII Century*
Cartouche-form mirror with scrolled and shell-carved frame crested
by a panache.   *Height, 28½ inches; width, 18 inches*

176. PAIR CARVED AND GILDED ALTAR CANDLESTICKS
Italian, XVI Century
Knopped and leaf-balustered shaft carved with festooned cherub heads,
on trilateral leaf-scrolled base; fitted for electricity.
Height, 37½ inches

177. CARVED WALNUT CLAW-AND-BALL-FOOT CHILD'S CHAIR
Georgian Style
Back and seat in green worsted brocade; shell-carved cabriole legs and
claw and ball feet.

178. DECORATIVE PAINTING   *Italian School, XVIII Century*
Figure of the Sybil in voluminous green robes, writing with a quill upon
a tablet.   *Height, 24 inches; width, 18 inches*

179. PAIR CARVED WALNUT ARMCHAIRS   *Italian Régence Style*
Cartouche-shaped carved back and cabriole frame; back panel and
seat in gold brocade.

180. CHARLES II FINELY CARVED WALNUT CANE-BACK ARMCHAIR
English, XVII Century
Square doubly-paneled cane back with spiraled uprights supporting a
crowning rail beautifully carved with floral scrollings and amors flank-
ing a crowned double-headed eagle; open serpentine arms, spirally
turned and blocked legs and H-stretcher. With restorations.

181. ACAJOU COMMODE MOUNTED IN BRONZE DORÉ, AFTER BENEMAN
Louis XVI Style
With straight front and incurvate returns; fitted with drawers and
sliding trays concealed by a paneled cupboard with oval medallion
appliqué with a military trophy; paw feet. White tapestry marble top.
Height, 37½ inches; length, 6 feet 2 inches

28

[NUMBER 182]

182. PAIR LOUIS XV CARVED WALNUT AND
CELADON SILK MOIRÉ BERGÈRES
Molded horseshoe back with floral cresting and small armpads, the
serpentine arm supports curving down to meet a serpentine flower-
carved seat rail; cabriole legs. Back and seat cushion covered in pale
green *moiré* silk. With restorations.

[See illustration]

183. CARVED AND GILDED MARQUISE IN GENOESE JARDINIERE VELVET
Louis XV Style
Rococo carved love seat with cabriole legs, the back, sides and seat
cushion covered in fine old Genoese jardiniere velvet, somewhat worn.
Length, 47 inches

184. CARVED, GILDED, AND POLYCHROMED SIDE TABLE AND ALTAR
Spanish Renaissance
Table with leaf-carved top inset with red porphyrine marble; two
frieze drawers carved with scrolling leafage; on spiraled and vine-
carved columnar supports. Altar carved with panels of leaf scrollings
and *putto* figures. Both are reconstructed pieces. [Lot.]
Height of table, 30 inches; length, 38 inches

29

185. CARVED AND GILDED ARMORIAL PRIE-DIEU

Richly carved with a cherub head and garlands surrounding an escutcheon; covered in indigo *ciselé* velvet.

Height, 34½ inches; width, 24½ inches

186. PAIR SMALL CHINTZ-COVERED ARMCHAIRS *William and Mary Style*

Seat and arched back covered in yellow flowered chintz; open outscrolled arms, quadrangular cabriole legs. Mahogany finish.

187. THREE CARVED AND GILDED STATE CHAIRS IN GREEN CUT VELVET

Louis XIV Style

Scrolled cabriole frame carved with female mascarons upon the arms; back and seat in fine sage green cut velvet.

188. LOUIS XVI INLAID ACAJOU AND TULIPWOOD COMMODE
FINELY MOUNTED IN BRONZE DORÉ

Oblong top with tablet of *rouge de Flandre* marble, front with three small drawers paneled with *bronze doré* leaf *rinceaux*, surmounting two long drawers divided into three panels ornamented with appliqué vases of flowers and a musical trophy; round tapering legs.

Height, 34¼ inches; length, 51 inches

[See illustration]

189. INLAID ACAJOU LIBRARY TABLE, MOUNTED IN BRONZE DORÉ

Régence Style

Shaped top covered in tooled leather and rimmed in bronze; three drawers; cabriole legs. Mounted with *bronze doré* female mascarons, panels, handles, and paw feet.

Height, 31 inches; length, 5 feet 10 inches

190. CARVED OAK CRÉDENCE *French Gothic Style*

With doors and small cupboard richly carved with armorial devices and niches with figures of a knight in armor, the Angel and Virgin of the Annunciation. *Height, 57 inches; width, 45 inches*

191. FRENCH RENAISSANCE FORGED IRON FIRE SCREEN

With a *fleurdelisé* trellis and crested by three lilies.

Height, 42½ inches; length, 56 inches

[NUMBER 188]

EARLY YUNG CHÊNG ROSE VERTE PLAQUE: NUMBER 358

192. CARVED WALNUT CASSONE   *Veronese Renaissance*
With oblong sarcophagus top, the front panel carved with *putti* and
3 5 ~ leaf scrollings centring an escutcheon, the pilasters with winged female
figures; spirally gadrooned base on lion-paw feet. Reconstructed.
Height, 26 inches; length, 5 feet 10 inches

193. DECORATIVE OIL PAINTING   *After Titian*
2 5 ~ Reclining Danaë, after the well known painting in the Museo Na-
zionale, Naples.   *Height, 49 inches; length, 69½ inches*

194. PAIR WROUGHT IRON TORCHÈRES   *Spanish Gothic Style*
Tripod *torchère* with two coronets and supporting ten lights; fitted for
2 0 electricity.   *Height, 7 feet 6 inches*

195. PAIR ELABORATELY CARVED, GILDED, AND POLYCHROMED BEDSTEADS
Spanish Baroque
8 0 Footboard paneled and carved with baroque scrollings of acanthus
leafage and supported by leaf-scrolled brackets with winged cherub
figures; headboard with elaborate arched and scrolled acanthus cresting, richly gilded and surmounted by cherubs supporting a crown;
carved side rails to match. With box springs and mattresses.
Height, 6 feet; width, 5 feet

[See illustration of one]

196. CARVED AND GILDED LECTERN   *Spanish, XVII Century*
56 Elaborate baroque-scrolled and leaf-carved folding X-support, fringed
2 2 — leather reading tablet; in front is a pendent escutcheon. Together with
a carved tripod table in the rococo style. [Lot.]
Height of lectern, 56 inches; width, 22½ inches

197. BAROQUE ELABORATELY CARVED, GILDED, AND PAINTED COMMODE
Massive cartouche-form commode, richly carved with baroque scroll-
5 5 ~ ings and cartouche frames painted with nosegays of flowers in colors
on green grounds; contains a single cupboard.
Height, 53½ inches; length, 5 feet 3 inches

198. CARVED WALNUT AND JACQUARD TAPESTRY BENCH *James II Style*
5 0 Covered in machine-woven floral tapestry; bulb-turned legs with arched
2 2 and scrolled stretchers.   *Length, 5 feet*

32

[NUMBER 195]

199. THREE CARVED OAK AND WALNUT TALL-BACK ARMCHAIRS
Charles II Style

10 5 With spirally turned frames, the frontal stretcher and crowning rail carved with *putti* supporting an urn of flowers. One in walnut with crimson velvet seat and back panel; two in oak, caned and with velvet seat cushions.

200. CARVED WALNUT REFECTORY BENCH *Italian Baroque*

22 15 With pierced and scrolled skirt and six vase-turned legs with box-stretcher. *Length, 8 feet 1 inch*

201. PAIR ELABORATELY CARVED AND GILDED STATE CHAIRS
Venetian XVII Century Style

20 Seat and cartouche-form back in green silk damask, crested with a mascaron and scrollings of vines, the arms supported by seated satyrs; carved cabriole legs.

202. ACAJOU VITRINE MOUNTED IN BRONZE DORÉ *Louis XV Style*

35 With glazed door and sides and mirror back; cabriole legs. Richly mounted with *bronze doré* festoons, amoristic medallions, etc.
Height, 5 feet 10 inches; width, 32½ inches

203. PAIR CARVED AND GILDED STANDING LANTERNS *Spanish Baroque*

30 Shaft wrapped in green velvet and supporting a trilateral lantern richly carved with cherub heads and baroque scrolls and having oval glasses; fitted for electricity. *Height, 8 feet 6 inches*

203A. CARVED AND GILDED COFFER *Spanish Renaissance*

20 The front and sides carved with cherubs and heavy floral swags, centring a painted medallion of the Deposition of Christ.
Height, 26 inches; length, 39 inches

204. CARVED AND GILDED CURULE CHAIR AND TWO TABOURETS

60 X-chair and stool covered in antique floral brocade; and carved cabriole-leg stool in jardiniere velvet. [Lot.]

205. TURNED WALNUT AND CRIMSON VELVET BENCH
Cromwellian Style

17 15 Covered in garnet velvet; on six spool-turned legs with H-stretchers.
Length, 5 feet 1 inch

206. BRASS SALUTING CULVERIN

55 Mounted on swivel support. *Length, 48 inches*

34

207. PANOPLY OF POLE ARMS AND ARMOR
Comprising eight halberds, bills, and partisans; a morion; a Japanese chain mail and horn cuirass; a Japanese long sword in carved ivory sheath; and a flintlock gun with damascened stock. [Lot.]

208. PANOPLY OF POLE ARMS AND ARMOR
Comprising six halberds and two partisans, exhibiting an interesting variety of blades; a crossbow, a burgonet, and a pointed shield. [Lot.]

209. PANOPLY OF SWORDS AND ARMOR
Four swords of Gothic type, three with scrolled guards and one with cup hilt; a decorative Persian double-bladed axe; a Persian chased target shield; three war axes; and war cap with chain mail. [Lot.]

210. PANOPLY OF SWORDS AND ARMOR
Four basket-hilted and two cup-hilted swords; a cuirass, cabasset, gorget, pair of gauntlets, and pointed shield in the Renaissance style. [Lot.]

211. LOUIS XIV BRONZE FIRE GUARD
With serpentine railed front and vase finials.   Length, 58 inches

212. PAIR BRONZE DORÉ AND CRYSTAL GLASS CHANDELIERS
In the shape of a bowl of cut glass beads ornamented with gilded bronze mascarons; six scrolled arms for hanging lights, with beaded glass globes.   Diameter, about 32 inches

213. CHINESE GILDED BRONZE AND ENAMEL JARDINIERE
Enameled with scrollings of lotus blossoms in blue and turquoise; on five-legged stand.   Diameter, 14½ inches

214. THREE SANCTUARY LAMPS   Italian Baroque
One triangular, in carved and gilded wood; the other two in repoussé metal, hung with chains. As exhibited. [Lot.]

215. FOUR BRASS AND COPPER UTENSILS
Ajouré brass warming pan, bellows, and repoussé copper kettle and hanging jardiniere. [Lot.]

[END OF FIRST SESSION]

[NUMBER 254]

PASSEMENTERIE, DAMASKS AND BROCATELLES
IMPORTANT GOTHIC AND RENAISSANCE VELVETS
WITH NEEDLEPAINTING

216. EIGHT PAIRS CRIMSON SILK TASSELS   *Italian, XVII Century*
With knotted and fringed skirts, some trimmed with gold thread; in-
cluding two pairs of fine tassels with gold *passementerie* pendants.
[Lot.]

217. THREE LENGTHS OF BI-COLORED SILK FRINGE
                            French and Italian, mainly XVIII Century
Two lengths of crimson and white knotted fringe; one in green, white,
and yellow; four pieces. [Lot.]   *Total length, about 16½ yards*

218. FOUR LENGTHS OF SILVER LACE   *French, XVIII Century*
Narrow edging lace with various scallop-shell designs. [Lot.]
                                Total length, about 56½ yards

219. TWO LENGTHS OF GOLD AND SILVER LACE
                            French and Italian, Late XVII Century
Patterned with baroque floral motives. [Lot.]
                                Total length, about 10½ yards

220. TWO LENGTHS OF CRIMSON SILK FRINGE   *Italian, XVIII Century*
Knotted fringe, in two shades of crimson. [Lot.]
                                Total length, about 14 yards

221. FOUR LENGTHS OF FRENCH AND ITALIAN GOLD AND SILVER FRINGE
Fine pieces; as exhibited. [Lot.]   *Total length, about 18 yards*

37

222. PAIR GOLD-, SILVER-, AND SILK-NEEDLEPAINTED ESCUTCHEONS

Italian, circa 1700

Gold coronet and canopy, surmounting figure of the Virgin worked in blue and red silks, supported by gold clouds, before a silver background.

From French & Co., Inc., New York

30

223. LENGTH OF GOLD GALLOON   *Italian, Late XVII Century*

Broad band galloon, patterned with an undulating baroque foliage pattern; forty-one pieces. This and the following two lots constitute an exceptional length of matched galloon. [Lot.]

Total length, about 146 *yards; width,* 3 *inches*

35

224. LENGTH OF GOLD GALLOON   *Italian, Late XVII Century*

Design of the preceding; thirty-nine pieces. [Lot.]

Total length, about 152 *yards; width,* 3 *inches*

50-

225. LENGTH OF GOLD GALLOON   *Italian, Late XVII Century*

Design of the preceding; forty pieces. [Lot.]

Total length, about 154 *yards; width,* 3 *inches*

47 50

226. EIGHT LENGTHS OF GOLD AND SILVER LACE

French and Italian, XVIII Century

An interesting collection, with rococo scallop shells, Directoire palm leaves, and other designs; nine pieces. [Lot.]

Total length, about 31½ *yards*

20

227. LENGTH OF SILVER FRINGE   *Italian, XVIII Century*

An exceptional quantity of matched fringe; nine pieces. [Lot.]

Total length, about 59½ *yards*

50
22

228. LENGTH OF GOLD GALLOON   *Italian Baroque*

Woven with a geometrical trellis pattern enclosing stellate rosettes; ten pieces. This and the following lot constitute an exceptional length of matched galloon. [Lot.]

Total length, about 75 *yards; width,* 2½ *inches*

30-

229. LENGTH OF GOLD GALLOON   *Italian Baroque*

Design of the preceding; thirteen pieces. [Lot.]

Total length, about 75 *yards; width,* 2½ *inches*

r5-

38

230. LOT OF ANTIQUE GOLD GALLOONS
In about six different patterns, as exhibited; fourteen pieces. [Lot.]
Total length, about 31½ *yards*

17 10

231. APPLE GREEN SILK AND GOLD BROCADE CUSHION COVER
Italian, Early XVIII Century
Damassé and brocaded with golden rococo scrolls and sprays of pastel-colored flowers.

15 -

232. PAIR BLUE AND WHITE FLOWERED SILK ARMORIAL CUSHIONS
Spanish, XVIII Century
Brocaded with an allover floral trellis design and appliqué with the escutcheon of a cardinal.

20

233. PAIR EMBROIDERED BLUE SILK DAMASK ECCLESIASTICAL COLLARS
AND AN ESCUTCHEON   *Spanish, XVIII Century*
Sky blue damask collars embroidered in silver and pastel silks with flowers; and an Italian escutcheon with date 1760. [Lot.]

7 10

234. PAIR CRIMSON SILK BROCATELLE ARMORIAL CUSHIONS
Italian, XVII Century
Crossbanded with broad gold galloon and centred with an appliqué escutcheon of a cardinal archbishop.

50 -

235. PAIR GREEN SILK DAMASK AND EMBROIDERY ARMORIAL CUSHIONS
XVII-XVIII Century
Paneled in ruby velvet, with appliqué embroidery escutcheon and green prelate's hat with *fiocci.*

30 -

236. PAIR DRAP D'OR AND CRIMSON VELVET EMBROIDERY
ECCLESIASTICAL COLLARS   *Spanish, Late XVI Century*
Crimson velvet ground inset with *drap d'or,* patterned with a trefoil and pair of leaves within a pinnacled border.

10 -

237. MOSS GREEN VELVET CUSHION   *Genoese, XVII Century*
In beautiful heavy deep green velvet, paneled with gold galloon.

30 -

39

238. MOSS GREEN AND RUBY VELVET ARMORIAL CUSHION

17 50

Centre in ruby velvet with appliqué gold-embroidered escutcheon; trimmed with silver lace and bordered with seventeenth century moss green velvet.

239. FINE GOLD-NEEDLEPAINTED AND APPLIQUÉ-EMBROIDERED ORPHREY

Italian, XVI Century

7 50

Five quatrefoil needlepainted medallions enclosing figures of saints, including SS. Nicholas, Peter, and John the Evangelist, alternating with appliqué-embroidered vases of lilies. Gold fringe.

Length, 5 feet 10 inches; width, 10 inches

240. FOUR ROSE CRIMSON SILK BROCATELLE PANELS

20

Italian, XVII Century

Woven with jardinieres and huge blossoms with curling leafage.

28 inches square

241. EMERALD GREEN VELVET COVER   *Italian, XVII Century*

50

Heavy *strié* green velvet; lined; corner cut.   *39 inches square*

242. GOLD APPLIQUÉ-EMBROIDERED CRIMSON VELVET TABLE RUNNER

Portuguese, XVII Century

40

Appliqué-embroidered in *drap d'or* on crimson velvet to a design of large skeleton palmettes, within frameworks of leafage, and pairs of pomegranates; gold fringe.   *Length, 8 feet 9 inches; width, 20 inches*

243. TWO FRAGMENTS OF AN ISPAHAN CARPET

Eastern Persia, Late XVI Century

30

Crimson ground, woven in blues, dark green, fawns, and yellow with lotus within frameworks supporting symmetrical branches of buds; gold galloon.   *Lengths, 51 and 28 inches; width, 22 and 12 inches*

244. GOLD-EMBROIDERED APPLE GREEN SILK COVER

Italian, Early XVII Century

10
2 2

Green silk embroidered with a border and corner nosegays of tulips, pinks, and wild flowers in colored silks amid leafage of gold and silver thread; gold lace galloon. Worn.

Length, 5 feet 8 inches; width, 42 inches

[NUMBER 245]

245. SUPERB GOLD-NEEDLEPAINTED PANEL, WITH VIGNETTES OF SAINTS
Italian, Early XVI Century
Worked with four central compartments enclosing circular medallions
of SS. John the Evangelist, Peter, Paul, and Andrew, in landscapes,
surrounded by mascarons, strapwork scrolls, and blossoms; within a
border of ten compartments with smaller vignettes of saints and
Biblical episodes; gold backgrounds and designs worked in gold and
colored silks.   *Height, 52 inches; length, 5 feet 3 inches*

[See illustration]

41

246. THREE GOLD APPLIQUÉ-EMBROIDERED CRIMSON CUT
VELVET VALANCES   *Portuguese, XVII Century*
40   Appliqué-embroidered with gold galloon and *drap d'or* to a design of
openwork blossoms and strapwork, upon a ground of crimson velvet
cut with Louis XIV floral patterns. Gold-fringed and scalloped at
base.   *Length, 6 feet; depth, 31 inches*

247. EMERALD GREEN VELVET PANEL   *Italian, XVIII Century*
Three widths, in fine condition.
60 -   *Length, 5 feet 2 inches; width, 40 inches*

248. APPLIQUÉ-EMBROIDERED AND NEEDLEPAINTED AMETHYST
VELVET ALTAR FRONTAL   *Spanish Renaissance*
Seventeenth century amethyst velvet, appliqué-embroidered with four
60   cartouches enclosing needlepainted figures of Apostles, enclosed by
pillars, and bands of Renaissance lilies.
Length, 6 feet 3 inches; depth, 25 inches

249. CRIMSON SILK DAMASK COVERLET   *Spanish, Early XVIII Century*
45   Satin ground woven with a Louis XIV design of large flowering
pomegranates within frameworks of paired openwork leaves; four
widths.   *Length, 7 feet 9 inches; width, 6 feet 10 inches*

250. APPLIQUÉ-EMBROIDERED MOSS GREEN VELVET ROBE
Italian, Late XVII Century
210 - Long-skirted robe, with hem, neck and cuffs appliqué-embroidered in
gold with lilies. Fine quality.
From *Keller & Co.*, New York

251. PAIR GOLD APPLIQUÉ-EMBROIDERED RUBY VELVET VALANCES
Spanish, XVI-XVII Century
60 - Appliqué-embroidered with gold galloon, with a design of strapwork
forming skeleton palmettes; gold fringe.
Length of each, 23 feet 6 inches; depth, 10 inches

252. TWO GOLD APPLIQUÉ-EMBROIDERED RUBY VELVET VALANCES
Spanish, XVI-XVII Century
35   Similar to the preceding.
Lengths, 22 feet and 18 feet; depth, 10 inches

253. MOSS GREEN VELVET COPE   *Genoese, XVII Century*
150   Lustrous green velvet, the orphrey and hood bordered with gold
galloon. In fine condition.   *Length, 9 feet 7 inches; depth, 55 inches*

254. SUPERB NEEDLEPAINTED AND GOLD-EMBROIDERED CRIMSON VELVET
ALTAR FRONTAL   *Italian, XVI Century*
Ruby velvet paneled in four compartments and embroidered with a
design of curving gold and silver branches terminating in lilies, each
compartment centring an oval needlepainted medallion of SS. Martin,
Christopher, Stephen, and Michael, in landscapes; webbed gold fringe
at base.   *Length, 6 feet 10 inches; diameter, 33 inches*

[See illustration facing page 37]

255. MYRTLE GREEN SILK DAMASK COVERLET
                                      Italian, XVII-XVIII Century
Satin ground woven with a design of large flowering pomegranates
enclosed within frameworks of leafage, the latter supported by
diapered areas; four widths.   *Length, 6 feet 3 inches; width, 6 feet*

256. GOLD-EMBROIDERED CRIMSON VELVET VALANCE
                                            Spanish, XVI Century
Crimson velvet embroidered in gold with narrow borders of lilies enclosing the inscription ORATE · P · NOBIS · B C R I · E C R I; gold fringe.
                           Length, 7 feet 6 inches; depth, 9 inches

257. JARDINIERE VELVET FRONTAL   *Genoese, XVII Century*
Three widths of velvet in polychrome colors cut to symmetrical designs of large palmettes with blossoms and floral baskets; bordered
with silver lace.   *Length, 5 feet 9 inches; depth, 28 inches*

258. JARDINIERE VELVET FRONTAL   *Genoese, XVII Century*
Very similar to the preceding.
                          Length, 5 feet 2 inches; depth, 28 inches

259. CRIMSON SILK BROCATELLE HANGING   *Italian, XVII Century*
Woven in satin with a large symmetrical design of clusters of three
peonies and leaves enclosed by frameworks of foliage; bordered and
paneled with gold galloon. Two widths.
                          Length, 9 feet 5 inches; width, 43 inches

260. CRIMSON SILK BROCATELLE HANGING   *Italian, XVII Century*
Similar to the preceding   *Length, 8 feet 7 inches; width, 43 inches*

43

[NUMBER 261]

261. FINE GOLD-, SILVER-, AND SILK-NEEDLEPAINTED PANEL
WITH BIBLICAL VIGNETTES   *Spanish, Early XVI Century*
Richly worked in gold and colored silks with four central panels enclosing vignettes of the Birth of the Virgin and the Birth of Christ,
and smaller medallions of S. Sylvester, surrounded by scrolled frames
and branches of Renaissance lilies. Bordered by six full-length figures
of SS. Peter, John the Baptist, Andrew, Paul, John the Evangelist,
and Bartholomew, within niches.

Length, 5 feet 3 inches; width, 43 inches

Companion to the following

[See illustration]

44

262. FINE GOLD-, SILVER-, AND SILK-NEEDLEPAINTED PANEL
WITH BIBLICAL VIGNETTES   *Spanish, Early XVI Century*
Similar to the preceding, the two central vignettes depicting the Presentation of the Virgin and the Adoration of the Magi.

Length, 5 feet 2 inches; width, 44 inches

Companion to the preceding

263. PAIR APPLIQUÉ-EMBROIDERED BLUE VELVET COLUMN HANGINGS
Spanish, circa 1600
Light blue velvet, appliqué-embroidered in yellow satin outlined with cordonnets with a late Renaissance design of floral vases, scrolling leafage, and strapwork, with plain end panels. Velvet of rare color.

Height, 9 feet; width, 22 inches

From French & Co., Inc., New York

264. PAIR CRIMSON VELVET HANGINGS WITH VALANCE
Italian, XVII-XVIII Century
Trimmed with gold galloon; lined and interlined. Valance scalloped and paneled with galloon. Gold fringe.

Length of hangings, 9 feet; width, 6 feet 6 inches
Length of valance, 11 feet 3 inches; depth, 27½ inches

265. LOUIS XV IVORY SILK AND GOLD BROCADE COPE
French, XVIII Century
Damassé ivory ground brocaded in gold and colored silks with a rococo design of cornucopiae, spiraled ribbons, and blossoms. Bordered and paneled in gold galloon, the hood fringed.

Length, 10 feet; depth, 58 inches

266. THREE GOLD APPLIQUÉ-EMBROIDERED CRIMSON WOOL
VELVET RUNNERS   *Portuguese, XVII Century*
Crimson wool velvet, appliqué-embroidered with *drap d'or* to a symmetrical design of openwork palmettes and rosettes within frameworks of lilies.

Lengths, 8 feet 5 inches, 8 feet 7 inches, and 10 feet 6 inches
width, 22½ inches

267. FINE POWDER BLUE VELVET COVERLET   *French, Late XVII Century*
Light blue velvet, with rich patina; bordered with gold galloon.

Length, 8 feet; width, 8 feet 4 inches

From French & Co., Inc., New York

45

268. Two Crimson Silk Damask Runners *Italian Baroque*
Satin ground, woven with a design of huge flowering pomegranates surmounting pairs of waving blossoms and leaves.
Length of each, 15 feet 4 inches; width, 37 inches

95

269. Three Crimson Silk Damask Runners *Italian Baroque*
Design of the preceding. [Lot.]
Length of two, 15 feet 4 inches; of one, 10 feet 2 inches
widths, 37 and 32 inches

80

270. Lyons Ruby Velvet Coverlet *French, XIX Century*
In two widths; bordered with wide gold galloon. Velvet of superb quality.
Length, 9 feet; width, 52 inches

75

271. Crimson Velvet Hanging, Appliqué-embroidered
with Escutcheon *Italian, XVII Century*
Fine quality velvet showing patina, appliqué-embroidered with a coroneted escutcheon worked in gold and *point d'Hongrie*, the crown inset with paste jewels, the escutcheon within a frame of leafage. Wide silver galloon. *Length, 7 feet 6 inches; width, 6 feet 6 inches*

210 -

272. Pair Silk Embroidery and Crimson Velvet Hangings
Italian, XVII Century
Composed of a broad border of yellow silk, appliqué in crimson velvet, outlined with tapes and embroidered in colored silks, to a design of large blossoms, palmettes, and floral baskets; and a fine Genoese crimson velvet panel. Lined and interlined.
Height, 10 feet 7 inches; width, 39 inches

70

273. Important Gothic Crimson Ferronnerie Velvet and
Gold-needlepainted Cope *XV-XVI Century*
Rich garnet red velvet, showing the patina and wear of age, *ciselé* to a design of pineapples and cusped Gothic frameworks; orphrey with Spanish Renaissance needlepainting in gold and shaded silks developing six full-length figures of the Apostles Paul, Andrew, Peter, John, Philip, and Thomas, within gold niches, the two end figures with escutcheons.
Length, 9 feet 3 inches; depth, 53 inches

510

[See illustration]

46

[NUMBER 273]

274. CRIMSON AND OLD GOLD BROCATELLE HANGING
Italian XVII Century Style

6 5 -

Old gold ground, woven in crimson satin with a Louis XIV design of palmettes surmounting pairs of cornucopiae and enclosed within pairs of curling leaves; four widths.

Length, 9 feet 2 inches; width, 6 feet 10 inches

275. GOLD APPLIQUÉ-EMBROIDERED CRIMSON VELVET HANGING
Italian, XVII Century

6 0 -

Ruby velvet re-appliqué with *drap d'or* to a design of huge coroneted ogivals of leafage, palmettes, and pairs of drooping lilies; wide gold galloon and fringe. Lined with green plush velvet.

Length, 10 feet; width, 6 feet 6 inches

8 5

276. GOLD APPLIQUÉ-EMROIDERED CRIMSON VELVET HANGING
Italian, XVII Century

Companion to the preceding.

277. VERY IMPORTANT GOTHIC DRAP D'OR BOUCLÉ CRIMSON CUT VELVET HANGING
Venetian, Late XV Century

Gold ground, woven with a sumptuous design in *cicelé* crimson velvet, *bouclé* in part with gold threads, and developing broad double ribbon ogivals supporting large Gothic pineapple motives, garlanded with blossoms heads and springing pairs of liliform carnation blossoms. The velvet has the rich patina of age and is in unusually good preservation. Three widths, forming a hanging of exceptional size.

950 -

Length, 9 feet; width, 5 feet 9 inches

[See illustration]

278. GOTHIC DRAP D'OR BOUCLÉ CRIMSON CUT VELVET PANEL
Venetian, Late XV Century

100 -

Matching the preceding.   *Length, 38 inches; width, 23 inches*

279. MOSS GREEN VELVET COPE   *Italian, XVII Century*

Of soft lustrous green velvet.   *Length, 8 feet; depth, 54 inches*

2 5 0 -

[NUMBER 277]

280. THREE PAIRS CRIMSON AND OLD GOLD SILK BROCATELLE HANGINGS
Italian, XVII Century

60

Rose crimson satin on an old gold ground developing a bold symmetrical design of leaf ogivals; worn; lined and interlined. Bordered with gold galloon, one pair with fringe.

Length of one pair, 10 feet 4 inches
length of two pairs, 7 feet 2 inches; width, 28 inches

281. TWO PAIRS CRIMSON AND OLD GOLD SILK BROCATELLE HANGINGS
Italian, XVII Century

40—

Matching the preceding.   *Length, 7 feet 7 inches; width, 28 inches*

282. PAIR GREEN SILK DAMASK AND JARDINIERE VELVET HANGINGS
AND A VALANCE   *Italian, XVII Century*

50

Light green damask woven with a satin design of huge pomegranates enclosed within pairs of leaves; bordered on one side with a jardiniere velvet panel of red roses and green leafage on an ivory ground. Gold galloon and fringe. Lined and interlined. Scalloped valance. [Lot.]

Length, 8 feet 4 inches; width, 56 inches
Length of valance, 10 feet; depth, 22 inches

283. CHINESE EMBROIDERED FLAME RED SATIN COVERLET OF
IMPORTANT SIZE   *Circa 1800*

6√

Lavishly worked in shaded pastel silks with vignettes of landscapes with trees and lakes and numerous figures of children playing, centred with a summer pavilion; with a valance of green satin, also embroidered with children playing.

Length, 10 feet 4 inches; depth, 8 feet 4 inches

284. CRIMSON VELVET COVERLET   *Genoese, XVII Century*

Paneled with gold galloon; a portion of later date.

5√

Length, 7 feet 4 inches; width, 6 feet 6 inches

285. EMERALD GREEN SILK DAMASK COVERLET   *Italian Baroque*

Satin ground, woven with a Louis XIV design of large ogivals of openwork leafage enclosing flowering pomegranates. Five widths. Fine quality.   *Length, 9 feet; width, 8 feet 10 inches*

9√

[NUMBER 286]

286. APPLIQUÉ-EMBROIDERED SAPPHIRE BLUE VELVET HANGING

Spanish, circa 1600

Rich blue velvet, showing patina of age, appliqué-embroidered in fawn silk and gold thread with a late Renaissance design of strap scrollings and curving stems of lilies, centring a circular medallion of a Sun in Splendor. Velvet of rare color.

Length, 7 *feet* 6 *inches; width,* 6 *feet* 9 *inches*

From French & Co., Inc., New York

[See illustration]

51

287. PAIR RUBY VELVET COLUMN HANGINGS   *Genoese, XVII Century*
/ 2 0 -   Bordered with wide gold galloon, and fringed. Rich, heavy velvet.
Lined and interlined.   *Length, 8 feet; width, 25 inches*

288. PAIR RUBY VELVET COLUMN HANGINGS.   *Genoese, XVII Century*
/ 4̸0 -   Similar to the preceding. Lined and interlined.

289. GOLD APPLIQUÉ-EMBROIDERED CRIMSON VELVET VALANCE, WITH
THE ROYAL SPANISH BOURBON ARMS   *Spanish, Late XVII Century*
6 ſ ̄   Rich appliqué embroidery developing vines of lilies and rosettes, centring a coroneted escutcheon, flanked by pillars, and with a coroneted
escutcheon at each end. Gold galloon and fringe.
Length, 10 feet 2 inches; depth, 23 inches

290. EMPIRE GOLD-EMBROIDERED CRIMSON VELVET BALDACCHINO
Italian, circa 1810
3 0 0 -   Sumptuously worked in gold with a broad double border of leaf scrollings, blossoms, and anthemia, centring large appliqué escutcheons.
Length, 13 feet; width, 11 feet 6 inches

291. FIVE PAIRS CRIMSON SILK DAMASK HANGINGS
Italian, XVIII Century
/ / 0   Satin ground *damassé* with a naturalistic design of waving blossoms;
lined and interlined.   *Length, 11 feet; width, 5 feet 2 inches*

292. TWO LENGTHS OF CRIMSON SILK DAMASK AND A TABLE COVER
Italian, XVIII Century
4̸0   Design of the preceding; table cover with gold galloon. [Lot.]
Total length of two pieces, 24 feet 9 inches; width, 31 inches
Length of cover, 6 feet; width, 32 inches

293. LENGTH OF ROSE CRIMSON VELVET   *XVII-XVIII Century*
ſſ   Comprising eight pieces, as exhibited. [Lot.]
Total length, about 16 yards

294. LOT OF ANTIQUE GREEN VELVET
/ 0 0 -   Ten pieces of varying sizes, as exhibited. [Lot.]

52

GILDED AND POLYCHROMED WOOD CARVINGS AND
TERRA COTTAS OF THE XV TO XVII CENTURIES

295. FOUR CARVED, GILDED, AND POLYCHROMED CORBELS

Spanish, Late XVI Century

Gilded brackets supported by a full-length robed figure of one of the
four Fathers of the Church.   *Height, about 12 inches*

296. CARVED AND POLYCHROMED HAUT RELIEF OF THE ADORATION OF
THE MAGI   *Italian, XVI Century*

Depicting the Holy Family surrounded by the figures of the Three
Kings with their offerings and attendants. Imperfect. Framed.

Height, 19 inches; length, 36 inches

297. CARVED AND GILDED MONSTRANCE   *Spanish, XVII Century*

Figure of a winged angel surmounted by a sun in glory, supported by
four cherubs; on voluted trilateral base carved with cherub heads.

Height, 29 inches

298. WHITE-GLAZED TERRA COTTA GROUP OF THE VIRGIN AND CHILD

Italian, XVI Century

Standing figure in voluminous robes and hooded cloak caught up with
the left hand; holding the nude Child upon her right arm. With vel-
vet-covered plinth.   *Height of group, 24½ inches*

[See illustration facing page 64]

299. THREE CARVED, GILDED, AND POLYCHROMED STATUETTES IN
RENAISSANCE SHRINE   *French, XVI Century*

Figure of the Virgin and Child flanked by S. Gervais and S. Prothais,
wearing crowns and scarlet cloaks; in portico-form tabernacle with
round columns.   *Height, 27 inches; width, 25½ inches*

300. CARVED, GILDED, AND POLYCHROMED HAUT RELIEF

Spanish, XVI Century

Christ denied by Peter before the walls of the city, with spectators and
a cock crowing above the head of the kneeling apostle.

Height, 37½ inches; width, 21 inches

53

[NUMBER 301]

301. PAIR CARVED, GILDED, AND POLYCHROMED STATUETTES
Spanish, XVI Century

130- Figures of monkish saints in richly gilded white robes and indigo blue
coats, one holding a church and chalice, the other a missal and mar-
tyr's palm with three crowns. With gilded stands.

Heights, 43 and 41½ inches

[See illustration]

54

302. CARVED, GILDED, AND POLYCHROMED WALL SHRINE
Spanish, Late XVII Century
Arched and glazed cabinet bordered with gilded rococo scrollings and cherub heads. Together with a small group of the Madonna and Child in the canopied interior.   *Height, 26 inches*

303. PAIR GREEN GLAZED FAÏENCE BAS RELIEFS
South German or Swiss, Late XVI Century
Figures of Mars and Flora with sword and cornucopia, respectively, within arched niches with cherub-head spandrels; invested with a deep cucumber green glaze. Both repaired. Framed.
Height, 32 inches; width, 21½ inches

304. CARVED, GILDED, AND POLYCHROMED STATUETTE OF POPE GREGORY
Spanish, XVI Century
Standing figure in white robes and red-lined golden cloak with papal tiara, holding an open missal; in painted and gilded tabernacle.
Total height, 40½ inches; width, 19 inches

305. CARVED AND GILDED STATUETTE   *Italian, XVII Century*
Standing angelic figure wearing golden robes caught up to the knees, the left arm (restored) raised high; carved base.   *Height, 35 inches*

306. CARVED, GILDED, AND POLYCHROMED GROUP, IN SHRINE
Spanish, circa 1700
Figure of the Virgin in gold-brocaded black robe and richly brocaded and flowered white cloak, holding the nude Child upon her left arm. In rococo carved and gilded shrine ornamented with figures of pelicans and backed with green velvet.
Total height, 44½ inches; width, 21 inches

307. CARVED, GILDED, AND POLYCHROMED STATUETTE OF S. BARBARA
Spanish, XVI Century
Standing robed and cloaked figure holding an open missal, with her tower at her left side, the face re-colored; on round base.
Total height, 25 inches
From L. Salomon, Paris, 1909

55

[NUMBER 308]

308. LATE GOTHIC CARVED, GILDED, AND POLYCHROMED STATUE OF
     S. GEORGE   *Spanish, Late XI' Century*

450 — Standing figure of the knight in armor wearing a gilded white cloak
     and holding aloft a sword (restored); beneath his feet lies the dragon
     of Evil, in whose grasp is a tub containing a small child, emblematic
     of Innocence.   *Height, 5 feet 4 inches*

                    [See illustration]

56

[NUMBER 309]

309. CARVED, GILDED, AND POLYCHROMED HAUT RELIEF
     IN GILDED TABERNACLE   *Spanish, XVI Century*
     Depicting the Adoration of the Infant Christ in the manger, with the
     Holy Family and shepherds, together with the ox and the ass grouped
     around the nude Child. Re-colored and mounted in Gothic type richly
     carved and gilded tabernacle.

                    Height, 6 feet 1 inch; width, 44½ inches

     [See illustration]

57

310. TERRA COTTA GROUP OF THE VIRGIN AND CHILD
IN CARVED AND GILDED SHRINE   *Italian Renaissance*
Half-length figure of the Virgin with the standing figure of the nude
Child held against her right shoulder; in tabernacle with spirally
twisted vine-carved columns surmounted by a cresting of cherubs sup-
porting a cartouche.   *Total height, 43½ inches; width, 33 inches*

311. PAIR CARVED, GILDED, AND POLYCHROMED TORCHÈRE FIGURES
Spanish or Italian, XVII Century
Robed and gilded winged figure of an angel holding a spirally fluted
cornucopia; on leaf-carved plinth.   *Total height, 41½ inches*

312. GILDED AND POLYCHROMED PASTIGLIA BAS RELIEF
Italian, XV Century
Half-length figure of the Virgin in golden cloak and greenish blue
robe, holding the Child; in Renaissance tabernacle frame.
Height, 23½ inches; width, 24 inches

313. NINE PANELS OF LATE GOTHIC CARVED AND GILDED TRACERY
French and Spanish, XV-XVI Century
Charming fragments of flamboyant and other late Gothic fenestral
tracery, as exhibited. [Lot.]

314. CARVED AND POLYCHROMED TONDO   *Spanish, Early XVII Century*
Madonna and Child with cherub heads, and two cherubs supporting a
crown, enclosing a hanging pendant with carved figure of a *putto* amid
acanthus scrollings. Together with a companion pendant.
Diameter, 36 inches

315. CARVED, GILDED, AND POLYCHROMED STATUE OF THE
MADONNA AND CHILD   *Spanish, Late XVI Century*
Standing figure of the Virgin in loosely draped voluminous hooded
robe of gold edged with greenish blue, holding the nude Child in her
arms.   *Height, 40½ inches*

316. PAIR CARVED, GILDED, AND POLYCHROMED TORCHÈRE FIGURES
Italian, Late XVI Century
Standing robed figure in short gilded corselet and flowing cloak,
winged, and holding a cornucopia fitted for electricity; on voluted
plinth carved with a cherub head.   *Height, 37 inches*

[NUMBER 317]

317. IMPORTANT LATE GOTHIC CARVED, GILDED, AND
       POLYCHROMED GROUP   *Spanish, XVI Century*
       Mounted figure of S. James, upon a rearing white horse; robed in
       polychromed and gilded corselet and wearing a wide-brimmed hat, the
       hat and saddle trappings ornamented with the pilgrim's scallop shell,
       his emblem. Beneath the feet of the horse lies the recumbent figure of
       a man in red and green robes, endeavoring to protect himself with a
       shield. The upraised weapon in the right arm of the saint is missing.
       The base is in three parts. The group retains a rich and interesting
       coloration.   *Height, 43½ inches; width, 37 inches*
       From Nicholas Martin, New York, 1909

                         [See illustration]

                                59

[NUMBER 318]

318. SCULPTURED AND POLYCHROMED TERRA COTTA GROUP OF THE
VIRGIN AND CHILD   *Florentine School, XV Century*
Half-length figure of the Virgin in red robe and bluish green hooded
/ 2 5 0 - cloak, holding the nude Child upon a cushion; in polychromed and
gilded round-arched tabernacle frame.
Total height, 33 inches; width, 25½ inches

[See illustration]

319. TERRA COTTA BAS RELIEF OF THE VIRGIN AND CHILD
Attributed to Antonio Rossellino, Florentine: c. 1427-1478
/ / 0 - Half-length figure of the Virgin, holding the Child in her right arm.
Repaired. In round-arched tabernacle frame.
Total height, 44½ inches; width, 26¾ inches

[NUMBER 320]

320. GOTHIC FINELY CARVED, GILDED, AND POLYCHROMED
STATUE OF S. GEORGE   *South German*, circa 1500

Standing figure of the saint in gilded Gothic armor carrying a long
sword (restored) and wearing a high round cap; he stands astride a
black dragon. Base repaired. On carved, gilded, and polychromed
pedestal in the Gothic taste.

Height of statue, 45 inches; of pedestal, 46 inches

Collection of Oscar Hainauer, Berlin

Described in W. ʌ. Bode, *The Collection of Oscar Hainauer*, 1906,
p. 66, No. 42

[See illustration]

61

321. CARVED, GILDED, AND POLYCHROMED STATUE OF S. CLARA
Spanish, circa 1600

50 - Standing figure cloaked and hooded, in nun's robes with rich brocade
pattern in blue and red polychromy and gilding; gilded base.
Total height, 48 inches

322. PAIR RICHLY CARVED, GILDED, AND POLYCHROMED COLUMNS
Spanish, Late XVI Century

100- Gilded Corinthian column with richly carved and polychromed acanthus scrollings, the base with a cartouched cherub head and two bird
figures. *Height, 44 inches*

323. TWO PAIRS MAMMOTH CARVED, GILDED, AND
POLYCHROMED COLUMNS *Spanish, circa 1600*

45 Spiraled baroque columns, one pair carved with entwined blossoms, the
other pair with amors amid flowers and foliage; Corinthian capitals.
[Lot.] *Heights, 10 feet 3 inches, and 8 feet 9 inches*

STONE SCULPTURES OF THE XII TO XVI CENTURIES

324. SCULPTURED ALABASTER HAUT RELIEF FRAGMENT
Italian, XVI Century

40 Robed and hooded seated figure of the Virgin holding an open book
and instructing the nude Child; at her left, the infant S. John.
Height, 12 ¼ inches

325. SCULPTURED ALABASTER BENITIER *French (?), XVI Century*

20 Gadrooned stoup surmounted by a canopied Latin cross.
Height, 11 ½ inches

326. SCULPTURED MARBLE HAUT RELIEF *Spanish, XVI Century*

40 - Virgin of the Immaculate Conception supported by cherubs, with God
the Father and the Holy Ghost above, amid clouds and cherubs;
framed. *Height, 12 inches; width, 9 inches*

327. GOTHIC SCULPTURED LIMESTONE CRUCIFIXION GROUP
French, XIV Century

55 A crocketed Greek cross carved with bands of vermiculation; on one
side, the figure of the crucified Christ and, on the opposite face, the
standing cloaked and crowned figure of the Virgin. Imperfect.
Height, about 40 ½ inches

62

[NUMBER 328]

328. GOTHIC FINELY SCULPTURED LIMESTONE GROUP OF THE
     VIRGIN AND CHILD   *Ile de France, XV* Century
     Graceful standing robed and hooded figure of the Virgin wearing a
     crown and holding the Child in the curve of her left arm, the right
     forearm missing. Retains traces of old polychromy. *Height, 33 inches*

                    [See illustration]

                          63

[NUMBER 329]

329. SCULPTURED LIMESTONE STATUETTE OF A BISHOP
Normandy, Early XVI Century
Standing figure wearing mitre and cope and holding a missal in the left
hand, the right hand raised in benediction. *Height, 46 inches*
From Jules Michel, Paris, 1909

[See illustration]

[NUMBERS 333 AND 298]

330. GOTHIC SCULPTURED LIMESTONE STATUETTE OF S. BARBARA

Haut Rhin(?), XV Century

50

Standing figure in flowing robes caught up in the left hand, in which she holds a palm; in her right hand, a missal and, upon her long hair, a crown. Behind her appears her emblematic tower (repaired).

Height, 37½ inches

331. LATE GOTHIC SCULPTURED AND POLYCHROMED LIMESTONE GROUP OF THE VIRGIN AND CHILD   *South German, Early XVI Century*

Passed

Standing figure in tight-waisted red robe and blue and gold brocade cloak caught up with the left hand to support the Child. Head of Child missing.   *Height, 39½ inches*

332. GOTHIC SCULPTURED AND POLYCHROMED LIMESTONE GROUP OF THE VIRGIN AND CHILD, ON PLINTH   *French, XV Century*

150

Standing robed and hooded figure of the Virgin, her robes enriched with blue polychrome, her hood flowing from beneath a crown; holding the scantily draped Child in a seated posture upon her left arm, an apple in His left hand. Together with a hexagonal Gothic plinth, beautifully carved with fenestral tracery, with crocketed pilasters and niches, enclosing figures of saints, the centre one refitted with a carved and polychromed wood door.

Height of group, 47 inches; of plinth, 32½ inches

[See illustration opposite]

333. GOTHIC SCULPTURED LIMESTONE SHRINE   *French, XIV Century*

550

Pilasters of cluster form enclosing a shrine supported by a cherub head, the niche painted with blue polychrome; surmounted by a traceried and pinnacled canopy with high crocketed spire. In several parts, as exhibited.   *Height, 9 feet 6 inches; width, 21 inches*

[See illustration on preceding page]

334. RARE ROMANESQUE SCULPTURED LIMESTONE COLUMN

French, XII Century

150

Quadruple cluster column in two sections, on shaped base carved with scrolling leafage, the capital with quaint grotesque and bird figures, amid curling foliage, and flaring into an octagonal abacus. Repaired.

Height, 5 feet 11 inches

66

[NUMBER 332]

335. SCULPTURED ROSE MARBLE BIRD BATH   *Venetian Renaissance*
Gadrooned bowl carved with spread eagles alternating with eagle-
crowned mascarons; on fluted and acanthus-carved swelling column
with guilloche-carved square base. Column repaired.
Total height, 54 inches; diameter, 23 inches

20

336. PINK VERONA MARBLE COLUMN   *Italian Renaissance*
With carved limestone Corinthian capital and base. Chipped.
Height, 55 inches

20 -

STAINED GLASS

337. THREE SMALL STAINED AND PAINTED GLASS FRAGMENTS
XVI-XVII Century
Depicting the Virgin and S. Joseph, figure of a saint in landscape, and
a bust of a bearded man. [Lot.]   *Heights, 6¾ to 11½ inches*

45

338. TWO STAINED AND PAINTED GLASS ARMORIAL PANELS
German, Late XVI Century
Mortuary panel and fragment with shield and helm, the former with
animal supporters. [Lot.]   *Heights, 12¾ and 11¾ inches*

20 —

339. THREE SMALL STAINED AND PAINTED GLASS MEDALLIONS
Flemish, XVI-XVII Century
Circular medallion depicting S. Barbara with the tower, and a pair of
small square plaquettes of musketeers. [Lot.]
Heights, 8¾ and 7 inches

60 -

340. THREE STAINED AND PAINTED GLASS ARMORIAL ROUNDELS
Dutch, XVII Century
Pair of oval medallions with coats of arms, dated 1655 and 1659; and
a roundel with escutcheon bordered with scrolling leafage.
Heights, 9 and 11¼ inches

130

341. TWO STAINED AND PAINTED GLASS MEDALLIONS
Flemish, Late XVI Century
One depicting a coat of arms with cherub supporters, the other the
figure of a saint in yellow *grisaille* surrounded by an ovolo border.
Heights, 11¾ and 10¾ inches

8 0 -

342

343

344

342

344

[NUMBERS 342 TO 344 INCLUSIVE]

ERRATUM

The two small panels AT THE LEFT in the above illustration are incorrectly
numbered in the plate. For 342 read 344, and vice versa. The panels at
the right are correctly numbered.

335. SCULPTURED ROSE MARBLE BIRD BATH   *Venetian Renaissance*
Gadrooned bowl carved with spread eagles alternating with eagle-
crowned mascarons; on fluted and acanthus-carved swelling column
with guilloche-carved square base. Column repaired.
Total height, 54 inches; diameter, 23 inches

20

336. PINK VERONA MARBLE COLUMN   *Italian Renaissance*
With carved limestone Corinthian capital and base. Chipped.
Height, 55 inches

20 -

STAINED GLASS

337. THREE SMALL STAINED AND PAINTED GLASS FRAGMENTS
XVI-XVII Century
Depicting the Virgin and S. Joseph, figure of a saint in landscape, and
a bust of a bearded man. [Lot.]   *Heights, 6¾ to 11½ inches*

45 -

338. TWO STAINED AND PAINTED GLASS ARMORIAL PANELS
German, Late XVI Century
Mortuary panel and fragment with shield and helm, the former with
animal supporters. [Lot.]   *Heights, 12¾ and 11¾ inches*

20 -

339. THREE SMALL STAINED AND PAINTED GLASS MEDALLIONS
Flemish, XVI-XVII Century
Circular medallion depicting S. Barbara with the tower, and a pair of

6 6

13

341. TWO STAINED AND PAINTED GLASS MEDALLIONS
Flemish, Late XVI Century
One depicting a coat of arms with cherub supporters, the other the
figure of a saint in yellow *grisaille* surrounded by an ovolo border.
Heights, 11¾ and 10¾ inches

8 0 -

68

342

343

344

344

342

[NUMBERS 342 TO 344 INCLUSIVE]

342. TWO STAINED AND PAINTED GLASS PANELS
Swiss, Early XVII Century
One depicting the Crucifixion, with figures of the Marys beneath a
baroque arch; the other a rebus of Scriptural scenes with captions in
German and the date 1619, flanked by figures of *putti* holding shields.
Height, 13½ inches; width, 11 inches

[See illustration on preceding page]

343. STAINED AND PAINTED GLASS PANEL   *Swiss, Early XVII Century*
Painted with five small vignettes of religious subjects and two escutcheons supported by angelic figures within a Renaissance tabernacle
of later date with red and mauve columns, enclosed by narrow windows; with memorial captions in German. Some cracks. Framed.
Height, 21¼ inches; width, 18¾ inches

[See illustration on preceding page]

344. TWO STAINED AND PAINTED GLASS PANELS
Swiss, Early XVII Century
One depicting Abraham sacrificing Isaac, with the angel appearing
above in the clouds and the ram caught in a thicket; below is a caption
in German with the date 1629, flanked by escutcheons. The other
depicts an allegory of Truth overcoming the Deadly Sins, with three
niches below, each containing the figure of an angel holding a shield.
Height, 13¾ inches; width, 11 inches

[See illustration on preceding page]

345. STAINED AND PAINTED GLASS ARMORIAL PANEL   *Swiss, dated* 1639
Painted with an escutcheon with helm and leaf mantling, enclosed by
pilaster figures; cartouched and captioned in German below.
Height, 13½ inches; width, 12½ inches

346. STAINED AND PAINTED GLASS CASEMENT PANEL
German, Early XVII Century
Painted with an escutcheon surrounded by amors, vases of fruit, and
other Renaissance ornament, with a cartouche below captioned in
German.   *Height, 37 inches; width, 18¾ inches*

70

[NUMBER 348]

[NUMBER 350]

347. PAIR STAINED AND PAINTED GLASS PANELS   *Flemish, circa* 1600
Full-length figures, standing before a column, of the saintly Elizabeth,
prioress of Herenthal, and Gertrude, daughter of S. Elizabeth, painted
en grisaille in nun's robes, and carrying a spray of lilies, and a book
and candle, respectively; cartouches below captioned in Latin.
Height, 52 inches; width, 14½ inches

348. PAIR LEADED WINDOWS INSET WITH STAINED AND PAINTED GLASS
XV-XVI Century
Arched windows of leaded glass inset with assembled fragments, including a *Pietà*, various heads, and Renaissance ornament, with two
fine panels below, one depicting the Agony in the Garden, the other
the Annunciation to the Shepherds.
External height, 5 feet 1¼ inch; width, 20⅜ inches

[See illustration facing page 70]

349. PAIR LEADED GLASS CASEMENTS INSET WITH STAINED AND
PAINTED GLASS   *Flemish, Early XVII Century*
Each painted with a baroque cartouche flanked by clusters of lilies of
the valley and surmounted by an oval escutcheon with the arms of
Godfrey, Duke of Brabant and of Abbot Theodore Tulden (fl. 1463);
with cartouches so captioned in Latin.
External height, 40¾ inches; width, 27½ inches

350. PAIR LEADED GLASS CASEMENTS INSET WITH STAINED AND
PAINTED GLASS PANELS   *Flemish, XVII Century*
Depicting the lying in state of the saintly Bishop Norbert, surrounded
by white-robed monks and townsfolk, within the chapel; and the funeral
procession, with monks and bishops followed by noblemen carrying
candles. Below each appears a Renaissance cartouche captioned in
Latin and hung with swags of fruit.
External height, 6 feet; width, 27½ inches

[See illustration opposite]

73

[NUMBER 351]

351. GOTHIC STAINED AND PAINTED GLASS PANEL   *English, XV Century*
Depicting the figure of a knight in full armor on horseback, cantering
through a meadow, and a second kneeling figure, perhaps his squire,
also in full armor, at the right; before a ruby background scattered
with a yellow device resembling a stonemason's hammer; at the upper
corners are added *fleurs de lis*. Framed.

Total height, 26¼ inches; length, 28 inches

[See illustration]

74

[NUMBER 352]

352. GOTHIC STAINED AND PAINTED GLASS PANEL   *French, XIV' Century*
Standing figure of the Virgin in yellow robe and green-edged red cloak,
holding the Child, Who is robed in green and mauve, upon her left
arm; blue background with tile pattern, finished with an added edging
of Renaissance motives painted in golden yellow. Some cracks and
restorations.   *Height, 38 inches; width, 19 inches*

[See illustration]

75

[NUMBER 353]

353. IMPORTANT GOTHIC STAINED GLASS WINDOW   *French, XIV Century*
Depicting the standing figure of S. Matthias in blue and green robes
and golden cloak, holding his sword by its point, before a blue background; before a Romanesque round arch with border of leaves and
rosettes upon a ruby band. With some restorations to border. Framed.
External height, 37 inches; width, 19¾ inches

[See illustration]

76

[NUMBER 354]

354. RARE ROMANESQUE STAINED GLASS WINDOW
French(?), XIII Century

Tall narrow panel with very fine border of leafage in a brilliant blue
ground edged with ruby and enclosing three panels, each containing a
pair of figures: the first laying a head upon a charger, the second pre-
paring burial for a crucified figure, the third kneeling in prayer. With
some restorations. Framed.

External height, 56½ inches; width, 20 inches

[See illustration]

77

[NUMBER 355]

355. STAINED AND PAINTED GLASS WINDOW   *German, XVI Century*
Arched window, depicting the half-length figure of a female saint in brilliant red, blue, and mauve garments and carrying a cross, before a background of convent buildings and churches; above appears a Renaissance arch hung with a festoon; assembled border of fragments painted with *fleur de lis,* crowns, and royal monograms.

External height, 51½ inches; width, 32¾ inches

[See illustration]

78

356. FRENCH GOTHIC STAINED AND PAINTED GLASS WINDOW

Depicting one of the Magi kings in green robes and red cloak and mounted upon a white horse, making his way across open country at night, pointing to the sky in which the Star of Bethlehem is shining; Romanesque type ruby border of rosettes. Reconstructed piece.

Height, 32¼ inches; width, 27⅛ inches

110 -

357. FOUR STAINED AND PAINTED GLASS PANELS

Leaded green glass, comprising a pair inset with late fifteenth century escutcheons; and a pair with gold cornucopiæ of fruit, Flemish, early seventeenth century. [Lot.]

Height, 16½ inches; length, 20 inches
Height, 17½ inches; width, 14½ inches

70 -

IMPORTANT CHINESE PORCELAINS
MAINLY OF THE *K'ANG-HSI* PERIOD

358. ROSE VERTE PLAQUE   *Early Yung Chêng*

One of the earliest examples of *famille rose* porcelain. The deep plate is beautifully enameled with a cluster of rose, blue, and iron red lotus flowers with green foliage waving naturalistically; a humming bird swoops down from above.   *Diameter, 14 inches*

[See illustration facing page 30]

359. BLUE AND WHITE PLAQUE   *K'ang-hsi*

Painted in beautiful deep cobalt blue with a *mei hua* branch and a cluster of chrysanthemums amid rockery; diapered border with six floral reserves. Small repair.   *Diameter, 13¾ inches*

12

359A. PAIR THREE-COLOR FU-LION VASES   *Late K'ang-hsi or Yung Chêng*

Crouching figure of the lion in green and aubergine with curled yellow mane, supporting upon his back a quadrangular green vase reserved with painted Flowers of the Seasons. One repaired.

Height, 7¾ inches

200 -

360. PAIR FAMILLE VERTE OVOID VASES WITH COVERS   *K'ang-hsi*

Graceful slender oviform vase, the decoration divided into four compartments enameled with clusters of the four Flowers of the Seasons, separated by dotted green borders scattered with red and yellow plum blossoms; cap covers.   *Heights, 12 and 12½ inches*

[See illustration on following page]

79

[360]   [361]   [360]

361. FAMILLE VERTE PLAQUE   *K'ang-hsi*
     Depicting two exotic birds perched upon rocks amid flowering red and
60 — blue peonies and *mei hua* with rich green foliage. *Diameter, 14 inches*
                         [See illustration]

362. RARE FAMILLE VERTE PEACH PLATE   *Late K'ang-hsi*
     Deep plate of vitreous white porcelain, beautifully painted on the in-
60   terior with a single ripening peach bearing a gilded Shou character,
     the stems with delicate green leafage; on the exterior, three smaller
     unripe peaches, miniatures of the first. Six-character mark of the reign.
     Repaired.   *Diameter, 11½ inches*

363. BLUE AND WHITE PLAQUE   *K'ang-hsi*
17½   Painted in rich deep underglaze cobalt with a *fêng huang* bird and
     peony shrubs amid rockery.   *Diameter, 12¾ inches*

80

364. FAMILLE VERTE PLAQUE   *K'ang-hsi*

Painted with a phoenix amid red and yellow peony shrubs and *mei hua*
blossoms, perched upon a rock; diapered border with six reserves depicting the implements of the scholar.   *Diameter, 14 inches*

365. GREEN AND YELLOW POTTERY JARDINIERE   *Ming*

Quadrangular jardiniere with flaring sides, finely molded on the exterior with *Fu* dogs pursuing the brocade ball, and brown and yellow
lotus flowers amid green leafage, the corners with lotiform supports
and resting upon upturned bracket feet of the so-called bear's-paw
shape, joined by a valanced apron. Repaired. Has carved teakwood
cover.   *Length, 20½ inches*

[See illustration]

[NUMBER 365]

[NUMBERS 366 AND 367]

366. LANG YAO BALUSTER VASE   *K'ang-hsi*
Tall baluster-form body, rounding into a high incurvate neck and
clothed in a deep blood red glaze darkening gradually toward the foot
and beautified with a bold regular crackle; repaired. *Height, 18 inches*
Loan Exhibition, Duveen Bros., Inc., New York, 1907, No. 322

[See illustration]

367. LANG YAO JARDINIERE   *K'ang-hsi*
Deep bowl, coated on the exterior to within three-quarters of an inch
of the foot with a viscous furry glaze of clotted blood red color, the
interior in greenish white porcelain with a variable *café au lait* crackle.
Height, 7½ inches
[See illustration]

82

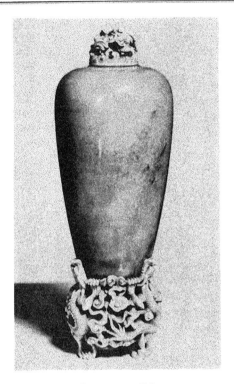

[NUMBER 368]

368. PEACHBLOOM AMPHORA, OF EXCEPTIONAL COLORING   K'ang-hsi
A magnificent specimen of the *p'in kuo hung,* with slender ovoid body,
but lacking the neck, which has been truncated. The paste is clothed in
a luminous peach pink glaze speckled with strawberry markings and
large areas of the coveted green mottlings representing the partially
ripened fruit. In point of coloring this vase is one of the finest speci-
mens in existence. Six-character *nien hao* of *K*'ang-hsi underfoot. Has
carved ivory cap cover and stand.   *Height, 5¾ inches*

From Thomas B. Clarke, New York, 1910
Loan Exhibition, Duveen Bros., Inc., New York, 1907, No. 327

[See illustration]

369. VERY IMPORTANT FAMILLE NOIRE BALUSTER-FORM VASE   *K'ang-hsi*
An important vase of the type called *yen yen,* with tall baluster-form
body and high cylindrical neck flaring at the mouth. The vase is coated
with a rich black glaze, the decoration being reserved in white and
painted on the biscuit in three colors—green, yellow, and aubergine—
in a design of tall mounting branches of peonies, magnolia blossoms,
and *mei hua,* amid which are flying birds, the shrubs springing from a
high mound of rockery, upon which are perched two *fêng huang.* The
vase shows traces of skilful repairs around the neck. The richness of
coloring and vigorous drawing of the decoration make this an important example of the period.   *Height,* 27⅜ *inches*

3500

[See illustration]

[NUMBER 369]

370. IMPORTANT FAMILLE NOIRE 'BLACK HAWTHORN' VASE   *K'ang-hsi*
Cylindrical club-shaped vase, with high tubular neck flaring at the lip.
The vase is coated with a black glaze exhibiting greenish iridesence and
reserved in shades of green and aubergine with rockery, from which
spring gnarled trunks bearing blossoms of the *mei hua* sketched in blue,
iron red, yellow, and sepia on the biscuit and reserved in the glaze;
birds are hovering above and are perched amid the branches. The vase
shows traces of a skilful repair on the neck. The coloring is unusually
varied and interesting.   *Height, 24½ inches*

[See illustration]

/600 ⌐

[NUMBER 370]

371. PAIR FINE FAMILLE NOIRE QUADRANGULAR VASES   *K'ang-hsi*

Club-form vase with square tapering body, flat shoulder, and high neck flaring at the lip. The vases are decorated on the biscuit with a flowering shrub upon each face, springing from a high mound of rockery—peonies, magnolias, and chrysanthemums in yellow, pale green, and aubergine with green leafage, reserved in the black ground. Upon the shoulder are scrolling stems of lotus flowers and, upon the neck, flowering shrubs and rockery, the whole reserved in three colors in grounds of shining black. Six-character *nien hao* of K'ang-hsi underfoot, penciled in underglaze blue.   *Height, 19 inches*

[See illustration]

[NUMBER 371]

372. FAMILLE VERTE BALUSTER-FORM VASE *K'ang-hsi*

Graceful baluster-shaped body with tall flaring neck, beautifully painted in the *famille verte* on-glaze enamels with a group of mandarins and warriors in a palace interior, outside which a procession descends a staircase leading to a rocky landscape appearing on the reverse, with pine trees and drifting clouds; upon the neck appear figures strolling in a pavilion garden, in a wooded mountain landscape. The shoulder exhibits four small landscape reserves on a diapered band. Neck repaired. A vase of exceptional brilliance of coloring.

Height, 27¼ inches

[See illustration]

175 -

373. FAMILLE VERTE TALL BALUSTER VASE *K'ang-hsi*

Baluster-form body with tall flaring neck, which has been truncated and reset at the shoulder. The vase is beautifully enameled in the lively colors of the *famille verte* with warriors on horseback galloping through a mountainous countryside wooded with pine trees; upon the neck, in a similar landscape setting, appear the figures of the Three Star Gods.

Height, 28¾ inches

[See illustration]

120 -

374. LANG YAO BALUSTER VASE *K'ang-hsi*

Tall baluster-form body with flaring neck, invested with a brilliant deep red glaze enlivened with a bold hairline crackle; repaired.

Height, 16¼ inches

100 -

375. FAMILLE ROSE PLAQUE *Ch'ing*

Enameled with a branch of *mei hua* blossoms and a pink peony, within a border with pink blossoms enameled upon a conchiform diaper with four floral reserves; repaired.

Diameter, 14 inches

90

K'ang-hsi
beautifully painted
of mandarins and
cession descends a
on the reverse, with
air figures strolling
age. The shoulder
of band. Neck re-

height, 27¼ inches

K'ang-hsi
been truncated and
ailed in the lively
rs back galloping
ne trees; upon the
ares at the Three

height, 28¼ inches

K'ang-hsi
a brilliant deep

. ht 16½, inches

Ch'ing
', within
aper with
14 inches

[NUMBER 372]

[NUMBER 373]

PAINTINGS

[NUMBER 376]

JEAN JACQUES HENNER
FRENCH: 1829-1905

376. MAGDALENE WEEPING

Profile kneeling figure to the right of a young girl with auburn hair and wrapped in a peacock green drapery, her upper body bare, weeping; brown background with an aperture showing a blue sky. Signed at lower left, J. HENNER.   *Height, 16½ inches; width, 13½ inches*

[See illustration]

92

[NUMBER 377]

ADOLPHE JOSEPH THOMAS MONTICELLI
FRENCH: 1824-1886

377. FÊTE CHAMPÊTRE

A group of female figures, some cloaked, some scantily draped, before a background of russet woodland. Signed at lower left, J. MONTICELLI.

Panel: Height, 18¾ inches; length, 39 inches

[See illustration]

SIR ANTHONY VAN DYCK (FOLLOWER OF)
FLEMISH SCHOOL

378. PORTRAIT OF A LADY

Bust-length portrait to half right of a lady with curled ringlets, wearing a crimson decolleté gown edged with gold. In elaborate baroque frame carved with huge acanthus scrolls.

Total height, 66 inches; width, 56 inches

93

[NUMBER 379]

SPANISH SCHOOL
CIRCA 1500

379. THE DEPOSITION, WITH FOUR SAINTS

Altarpiece divided into five panels, the central one depicting the Savior lowered into the tomb by two angels; flanked by figures of S. Barbara, S. Anne with the Virgin, S. Catherine, and S. Margaret. In elaborate tabernacle frame with carved and gilded Gothic fenestral tracery, within a border of undulating branches.

Panel: Total height, 32 inches; length, 77 inches

[See illustration]

SPANISH SCHOOL
XVI CENTURY

380. SCENES FROM THE LIFE OF THE VIRGIN AND THE PASSION: ALTARPIECE

Large predella divided into six panels depicting: The Pentecost, with the tongues of fire descending upon the Apostles; the Crucifixion; the Resurrection; the Assumption of the Virgin, Christ and Mary Magdalene in the Garden, and the Adoration of the Shepherds. Fine carved and gilded tabernacle ornamented with festoons, cherub heads, and pendants of fruit and military trophies.

Total height, 68½ inches; length, 75½ inches

[See illustration]

94

[NUMBER 380]

GIOVANNI BATTISTA TIEPOLO [Attributed to]
Italian: 1696-1770

381. Virgin and Child with Cherubs and Adoring Saints

The Virgin, in blue and rose robes and holding the nude Child upon her lap, is seated amid clouds surrounded by cherub heads; below appears the standing figure of S. Joseph in aubergine robe and golden cloak accompanied by a kneeling friar, perhaps S. Bernard, who gazes upwards in adoration. In fine carved, gilded, and polychromed Ionic tabernacle of the late Renaissance.

Total height, 110 inches; width, 65½ inches

[See illustration]

SPANISH SCHOOL
XV Century

382. Altarpiece with Three Saints

Full-length figure of S. Margaret flanked by two archangels, each within a Gothic niche with gilded mullions and pinnacles.

Panel: Height, 27 inches; length, 53 inches

JOSE DE RIBERA [Attributed to]
Spanish: 1588-1656

383. The Savior Blessed by John the Baptist

Figure of the saint, partly wrapped in a scarlet drapery, his right arm extended over the head of the youthful Savior; in the background two figures of women, with cherubs in the sky and clouds parting before the Holy Ghost. *Height, 82 inches; width, 54 inches*

From Nicholas Martin, New York, 1909

SOUTHERN FRENCH (OR SPANISH) SCHOOL
Circa 1500

384. The Twelve Apostles: Two Altarpieces

Two panels, each divided into three niches containing two figures of the apostles with their attributes, in costumes of reds, greens, and browns, before gold backgrounds with *bulino* work. Gilded tabernacle frames. *Height, 35½ inches; length of each, 83 inches*

[NUMBER 381]

TAPESTRIES

385. FLEMISH TAPESTRY VALANCE   *Early XVIII Century*
Woven in blues, greens, *tête de nègre,* and fawns, with clustered fruit
and flowers centring a small oval cartouche of roses.
Length, 6 feet; depth, 16 inches

386. LOUIS XVI AUBUSSON TAPESTRY PANEL   *XVIII Century*
JEU DE COLIN-MAILLARD. Two maidens and a youth are playing a
game of blind-man's buff before a wall, behind which is a vista of open
country with clumps of trees and a country house. Upper portions apparently of later date.   *Height, 7 feet; width, 43 inches*

387. WISMAR RENAISSANCE MILLEFLEURS TAPESTRY
Worked in richly varied colors on a dark blue ground with a profusion
of fruit and flowers amid leafage, centring a circular vignette depicting
the angels appearing to Abraham, before a landscape; border of fruit
and flowers, animals, and narrative vignettes flanked by allegorical
figures. Late example, possibly seventeenth century.
Height, 9 feet; width, 5 feet

[See illustration]

388. FELLETIN TAPESTRY HANGING   *XVIII Century*
Verdure landscape, with buildings in the background partly concealed
by the foliage of a tree; in the foreground is a fox.
Height, 6 feet 5 inches; width, 33 inches

98

[NUMBER 387]

389. BRUSSELS TAPESTRY PANEL   *XVII Century*

190-   Depicting a canopied niche, surrounded by foliage and enclosing a
statue of the Three Graces; a female figure with rose cloak is lifting a
basket of fruit as an offering. *Length, 8 feet* 9 *inches; width, 46 inches*

[See illustration]

FRENCH, SPANISH, AND ITALIAN FURNITURE
AND DECORATIONS

390. Tanagra Terra Cotta Group
Figure of Aphrodite riding on a triton.   *Height, 6¼ inches*
From Azeez Khayat, New York, 1903
[See illustration]

391. Tanagra Terra Cotta Group
Nude bearded figure of Bacchus bending over to assist the drunken
Silenus kneeling upon the ground.   *Height, 8¾ inches*
—From Azeez Khayat, New York, 1903
[See illustration]

[390]   [391]   [392]

392. Tanagra Terra Cotta Statuette
—Seated figure of a Greek maiden, drawing off her robe from her left
shoulder.   *Height, 6¾ inches*
[See illustration]

393. Hispano-moresque Copper Lustre Plaque   *Circa 1600*
Deep plaque with bossed cavetto surrounded by seven leaves painted
in copper lustre, the broad marli with molded and lustre foliations.
Diameter, 16 inches

394. FRENCH PEWTER PLAQUE, INSET WITH
— SIXTEENTH CENTURY LIMOGES ENAMEL MEDALLION
Round charger, probably of the eighteenth century, with bossed cavetto inset with a *grisaille* enamel medallion depicting a saint preaching. *Diameter, 17¼ inches*

[NUMBER 395]

395. URBINO MAJOLICA PLATE
ATTRIBUTED TO ORAZIO FONTANA   *Dated* 1548
THE ROMANS DEFEATING THE CARTHAGINIANS UNDER HANNIBAL.
Beautifully drawn scene with a lively cavalry battle raging in the foreground and, in the distance, a city upon the farther side of the river; in shades of blue, green, orange, yellow, and aubergine. Captioned on verso. Repaired. *Diameter, 10⅞ inches*
[See illustration]

396. URBINO MAJOLICA PLATE   *XVI Century*
THE STORY OF CURTIUS. The Roman hero in the foreground mounted on a white horse leaping into the chasm, surrounded by warriors; in the middle distance, a rocky landscape. Painted in the colors of the preceding. Repaired. *Diameter, 11 inches*

102

397. PAIR ADAM CARVED AND GILDED EAGLE SCONCES
In the form of bowknotted pendent tassels supporting two scrolled
arms for lights, surmounted by an eagle with crossed bow and arrow;
one imperfect.   *Height, 38 inches*

398. PAIR REPOUSSÉ SILVER SANCTUARY LAMPS
                                        Italian, XVII-XVIII Century
Elaborately shaped and gadrooned bowl terminating in a cauliflower
finial and hung by three chains from cherub supports.
                                        Height, about 40 inches

399. CARVED AND GILDED WALL MIRROR   *Spanish Baroque*
Upright, with border of carved and scrolled acanthus leaves.
                              Height, 22 inches; width, 17½ inches

400. MISSALE ROMANUM, BOUND IN VELVET WITH SILVER MOUNTS
                                        Padua, 1705
Missale Romanum ex Decreto Sacrosancti Concilii Tridentini. Folio,
printed in two columns in black and red, with passages of printed
music and fine full page line engravings; contemporary binding of
wine red velvet, mounted with *repoussé* silver medallions and corner
pieces of *ajouré* rococo floral ornaments.

401. ROMANESQUE GILDED BRONZE AND CHAMPLEVÉ ENAMEL
     PROCESSIONAL CRUCIFIX   *French, XIII Century*
Cross engraved with foliations and with appliqué figures of the crucified Christ, the weeping Marys, and other figures upon the arms;
ornamented with plaquettes of *champlevé* enamel reserved with rude
figures in bronze, a plaquette upon the back depicting God the Father.
                                        Height, 24¼ inches
[See illustration on following page]

402. ROMANESQUE BRONZE PROCESSIONAL CRUCIFIX
                                        French, XII-XIII Century
Rude figure of the Savior upon a *fleurdelisé* cross ornamented with
cabochon stones, most of which are missing; has stand.
                                        Total height, 24½ inches
[See illustration on following page]

103

[403]   [402]   [401]

403. REPOUSSÉ SILVER PROCESSIONAL CRUCIFIX   *Spanish, XVI Century*
Cross fleury *repoussé* with leaf scrollings and with quatrefoil plaquettes of the Savior and the allegorical figures of the Four Evan-
gelists, supporting a crucified Christ; on pierced and shell-molded
hexagonal support.   *Height, 27½ inches*
[See illustration]

404. CARVED AND GILDED CARTOUCHE WITH TALAVERA FAÏENCE
MEDALLION   *Spanish Renaissance*
Oval cartouche with a border of plateresque carving of monsters and
leaf scrollings; centring an inset plaque of Talavera faïence, depicting
a harvest scene.   *Height, 31½ inches*

405. PAIR CARVED AND GILDED CARTOUCHE-FORM WALL MIRRORS
                                       Spanish, XVII Century
Carved with strap scrollings and curling leafage and surmounted by a
Bérainesque canopy.   *Height, 36½ inches; width, 23½ inches*

104

406. CHINESE CARVED TEAKWOOD BIRD CAGE

Octagonal latticed cage with conical top, the borders, door and top carved with *ajouré* floral scrollings.   *Height, 25 inches*

407. INLAID ACAJOU BONHEUR DU JOUR, PLAQUÉ WITH PORCELAIN
                                                    French, XIX Century

Cabinet with double cupboard inset with amoristic and floral medallions of turquoise blue porcelain and with two small drawers; long drawer below, cabriole legs. Quartered, banded, and lavishly mounted in *bronze doré.*   *Height, 46 inches; width, 26 inches*

408. AUBUSSON TAPESTRY CARVED AND GILDED CANAPÉ AND
      PAIR FAUTEUILS   *Louis XV Style*

Cartouched back with shell and flower cresting, open arms with armpads, serpentine molded rails, cabriole legs. Covered in tapestry woven with cartouches of flowers on a gray ground, bordered with *vieux rose.*
[Lot.]   *Length of canapé, 6 feet*

409. PAIR AUBUSSON TAPESTRY CARVED AND GILDED FAUTEUILS AND
      PAIR SIDE CHAIRS   *Louis XV Style*

En suite with the preceding. [Lot.]

410. PAIR RÉGENCE CARVED WALNUT AND CRIMSON DAMASK ARMCHAIRS
          Southern French or Northern Italian, Early XVIII Century

Cartouche-form back, open arms with armpads and leaf-carved supports, shell carved rails and cabriole legs, scrolled H-stretcher. Back, seat, and armpads in crimson silk damask of the period.

411. PAIR RÉGENCE CARVED WALNUT AND CRIMSON DAMASK AND
      BROCATELLE ARMCHAIRS
          Southern French or Northern Italian, Early XVIII Century

Similar to the preceding; one in crimson damask, the other in brocatelle.

412. PAIR RÉGENCE CARVED WALNUT AND GREEN DAMASK ARMCHAIRS
          Southern French or Northern Italian, Early XVIII Century

Similar to the preceding, covered in seventeenth century green silk damask.

[NUMBER 413]

413. IMPORTANT LOUIS XV ACAJOU COMMODE, MOUNTED IN
BRONZE DORÉ

François Antoine Mondon (M. E. 1757); French, XVIII Century
Shaped oblong top with *brèche d'Aleppo* marble tablet of later date,
the front with three frieze drawers paneled with *bronze doré* guilloche
ornament and leaf *rinceaux,* surmounting two long drawers divided
into three square panels of ormolu and ornamented with *bronze doré*
garlanded escutcheons, ring handles with male and female portrait
medallions, and pendants of flowers upon the inner stiles. Chamfered
pilasters with appliqué figures of Bacchic satyrs, the pilasters terminating in cabriole legs. Stamped above both pilasters: F. A. MONDON, M. E.
Height, 35 inches; length, 50½ inches

Note: François Antoine Mondon, son and collaborator of the *maître ébéniste*
François Mondon, passed master in December, 1757, and worked in the rue du
Faubourg St. Antoine and, after his father's death, in the rue de Charenton, where
he was active until 1785. He is noted for his fine commodes. See Salverte, p. 229.

[See illustration]

106

414. LEATHER TRAVELING COFFER, FINELY MOUNTED IN BRONZE
English, dated 1686

Richly ornamented with appliqué baskets of fruit, nosegays of flowers and decorative patterns of bronze-headed nails, with initials ATP and the date 1686.   *Height, 23½ inches; length, 45 inches*
From Charles of London, 1912

415. RÉGENCE INLAID WALNUT BOMBÉ COMMODE
Northern Italian, Early XVIII Century

Serpentine oblong top, the front with three drawers, having rococo escutcheons and loop handles, and paneled with a banded cartouche; quadrangular cabriole legs.   *Height, 35½ inches; length, 53 inches*

416. GEORGIAN MAHOGANY CLAW-AND-BALL-FOOT CARD TABLE
American, XVIII Century

Oblong hinged top lined with brown baize, plain frieze with single drawer; quadrangular cabriole legs with claw and ball feet, the rear leg hinged as gate.   *Height, 29 inches; length, 31 inches*

417. NEEDLEPOINT AND CARVED BEECHWOOD LOVE SEAT *Louis XV Style*

Horseshoe back with seat cushion covered in floral *gros point*, with *petit point* cartouches depicting rustic lovers and a setter stalking deer; molded frame with cabriole legs.   *Length, 51 inches*

418. CARVED WALNUT AND CRIMSON BROCATELLE CANAPÉ
Northern Italian, Early XVIII Century

Arched and scrolled back, seat and outscrolled arms in crimson silk brocatelle, with bold Louis XIV floral design; shell-carved rails, cabriole legs. Dark patina.   *Length, 5 feet 10 inches*

419. ADAM CARVED MAHOGANY SWELL-FRONT SIDEBOARD
English, XVIII-XIX Century

Oblong, with convex kneehole front containing a fluted drawer flanked by deep drawers ornamented with fluting and festoons of husks; square reeded and tapering legs with spade feet.
Height, 36 inches; length, 5 feet

420. CARVED AND PARCEL-GILDED WALNUT VARGUEÑO
INLAID WITH BONE   *Spanish, circa* 1600
Chest with fall front elaborately *plaqué* with lock plate and diamond
medallions of pierced forged iron strapwork; opening to interior fitted
with numerous drawers and cupboards, parcel-gilded, ornamented with
spiraled bone colonnettes, and veneered with plaquettes of bone with
delightful engraved vignettes of vases of flowers, huntsmen and hounds,
arquebusiers, birds, rosettes, etc. On arcaded *puente* of the period,
with original straight and spirally fluted legs, the arcade restored. A
fine example.   *Total height, 58 inches; width, 41 inches*

[See illustration]

/o o

421. LOUIS XIV ACAJOU PENDULE AND GUÉRIDON
MOUNTED IN BRONZE DORÉ
Clock surrounded by *bronze doré* figures of sportive amors, on base
—ornamented with *bronze doré* floral festoons; on square tapering *guéri-*
don appliqué with a sun in splendor, pilasters, and classic ornament.
Total height, 7 feet; width, 19 inches

5 0

422. PAIR FRENCH RENAISSANCE FORGED IRON CHANDELIERS
Hexagonal, with *ajouré* voluted side members and supporting six
clusters of three arms for lights; fitted for electricity and suspended
from a coronet. Together with a small forged iron hexagonal
chandelier. [Lot.]   *Diameters, 6 feet, and 25 inches*

Passed

423. FOUR CARVED WALNUT AND GREEN BROCATELLE STATE CHAIRS
Italian XVII Century Style
Seat and high cartouche-form back covered in sage green brocatelle;
open voluted arms, leaf-carved and stretchered cabriole legs.

6 0

[NUMBER 420]

424. CARVED, GILDED, AND POLYCHROMED ALTAR WITH
WROUGHT IRON SCREEN   *Spanish, XVII Century*
The altar as a whole consists of three main sections, together with a
wrought iron grille fitted with a pair of gates and patterned with
voluted scrollings with cresting of lilies. The central section of the
altar is in the form of a three-tiered structure ornamented with spiraled
colonettes, caryatid pilasters, and niches enclosing small cupboards;
the side sections consist of two matched returns with spirally fluted
Corinthian columns carved upon the bases with polychromed leaf
scrollings and supported upon a frieze and paneled base richly carved
with acanthus scrollings; each of these returns also contains a central
niche for a statuette. The ironwork is of later date.
The whole is an assembled group in fine preservation and of unusually
decorative character; the frontispiece illustration shows the three main
constituents of the altar proper, together with a number of statuettes,
banners, and other decorative accessories, which do not form part of
the present lot.   *Height, 11 feet 6 inches*
From Nicholas Martin, New York

[See frontispiece]

425. GILDED AND POLYCHROMED CEILING, INSET WITH OIL PAINTING
                                        Spanish, XVII Century
Rectangular ceiling with polychromed borders of fruit and flowers and
inner border of fluting; the corners with blank baroque cartouches ornamented with cherub heads; surrounding a huge baroque scrolled cartouche edged with carved leafage, ornamented with sheathed figures
and clusters of fruit, and centring a tondo canvas depicting a nymph
and shepherd, flanked by two small oval medallion paintings. Executed
in wood and gesso, and in fine preservation.
                    Length, 23 feet; width, 10 feet 10 inches

From Nicholas Martin, New York

426. CARVED, GILDED, AND POLYCHROMED CRÉDENCE
                                        Spanish, XVI Century
Front cupboard and returns carved with niches containing figures of
the Savior bound to the column, and of SS. Peter and Paul, respectively, enclosed by turned pilasters and with cresting of cherub heads;
on four fluted and leaf-carved supports with back panel carved with
two figures of apostles. Apparently an assembled piece.
                    Height, 5 feet 1 inch; width, 34 inches

427. CARVED, GILDED, AND POLYCHROMED TABERNACLE
Italian, XVI Century
With dentiled triangular pediment, on fluted Corinthian columns, and
carved with cherub heads and borders of leafage; enclosing arched
panel covered in sixteenth century ruby velvet. Fine original example.
Height, 7 feet 2 inches; width, 5 feet 4 inches

428. PAIR CARVED, GILDED, AND POLYCHROMED PILASTERS
Italian or Spanish, Late XVI Century
Scrolled and richly carved with twin cherubs amid leafage, surmount-
ing angelic *torchère* figures. *Height, 6 feet 6 inches*

429. LOT OF CARVED, GILDED, AND POLYCHROMED CORBELS, ROSETTES
AND CHERUB FIGURES *Spanish Baroque*
Architectural fragments, including several cherub figures, some of the
period; two segments of curved architrave carved with pelicans and
leaf scrollings; seven winged ceiling rosettes, etc.; as exhibited. [Lot.]

430. COMPO ATRIUM TABLE *Roman Style*
Oblong top, on end supports with *adossés* winged lions enclosing an
anthemion. *Height, 33 inches; length, 6 feet 11 inches*

[END OF SALE]

III

Composition and Presswork
by

PUBLISHERS PRINTING COMPANY
William Bradford Press
NEW YORK

CPSIA information can be obtained
at www.ICGtesting.com
Printed in the USA
BVHW04*1141200818
525056BV00010B/532/P